The Philosophical Foundations of Christian Science

Mary Baker Eddy and her Radical Metaphysics

Nicholas Sheldon

James Clarke & Co.

James Clarke & Co.
P.O. Box 60
Cambridge
CB1 2NT
United Kingdom

www.jamesclarke.co
publishing@jamesclarke.co

Hardback ISBN: 978 0 227 18051 8
Paperback ISBN: 978 0 227 18045 7
PDF ISBN: 978 0 227 18044 0
ePub ISBN: 978 0 227 18046 4

British Library Cataloguing in Publication Data
A record is available from the British Library

First published by James Clarke & Co. 2025

Copyright © Nicholas D. Sheldon, 2025

All rights reserved. No part of this edition may be reproduced, stored electronically or in any retrieval system, or transmitted in any form or by any means, electronic, mechanical, photocopying, recording, or other-wise, without prior written permission from the Publisher (permissions@jamesclarke.co).

The Philosophical Foundations of Christian Science

Table of Contents

1. Beginnings — 1
2. Christian Science and Eddy's Metaphysical Idealism — 15
3. Eddy Viewed from Near and Far — 37
4. Robert Peel and the Conceptual Bridge — 47
5. The Philosophical Analysis of Christian Science — 57
6. Christian Science as a Philosophical System — 64
7. Christian Science Reframed — 81
8. Eddy's Radicalism: Problems and Solutions — 113
9. Criticism and Controversy: The Spanish Influenza and the COVID-19 Pandemic — 147
10. Penultimate Thoughts — 160

Bibliography — 167

Glossary — 175

Index of Subjects — 185

Index of Names — 188

Chapter 1

Beginnings

Overview

The nineteenth-century American, Mary Baker Eddy, is well known in the United States for having founded the religion Christian Science, but she is not generally regarded as a philosopher, let alone an original one.

Many factors may have contributed to history's mis-framing of Eddy. Her gender, the period in which she lived, and her notoriety in connection with the creation of a new religion made her appear non-conformal with the image of a philosopher. In the twenty-first century, interest has grown in the 'lost' female philosophers of history, although these figures have typically been overlooked due to their lack of visibility, rather than their prominence in another role. This book forms a part of the rediscovery of the contributions of female philosophers.

Eddy's Christian Science develops an empirical metaphysics which marries a radical form of idealism and scientific method by putting a priori metaphysical axioms to the test of experience. Christian Science's denial of the existence of illness, for which she is mostly known, is merely a fragment of a daringly ambitious, radical idealism denying the existence of matter and much more besides.

Eddy wrote in a nonlinear style, incorporating existing terms whose meaning she had redefined, making a careful restructuring and rephrasing of her work a necessary first step. Subsequent analysis of her system's internal consistency and its coherency reveals three potentially fatal flaws in her system of thought; a considerable part of the text therefore addresses these problems and offers possible solutions to them.

Mary Baker Eddy attained worldwide fame and notoriety in her lifetime, and, additionally to her system of thought, created in the Christian Science Church an international institution which still exists today. It is also true that her work, and that of people following in her footsteps, was and continues to be of great cultural significance, but despite the system which she created being underpinned by ideas very similar to the metaphysical idealism of certain German and British idealists, Eddy is not regarded as a philosopher in the same sense as the famous men of the eighteenth and nineteenth centuries; it is this injustice which this book both demonstrates and begins to rectify.

Although only publicly associated with healing, Christian Science asserts something quite remarkable considering its distance from academic philosophy: illness, suffering and the entire physical universe are not real, the only true reality being spiritual. The events which led Eddy to these and other highly counterintuitive conclusions will now be introduced.

The beginnings of a philosophical system

On 1 February 1866, a period in Eddy's life began in which she developed her own system of healing, initially with similarities to that of Phineas Quimby – a clockmaker turned hypnotist who developed a form of mental healing and who had briefly been her teacher[1] – but with a radical philosophical underpinning which went far beyond anything her mentor had considered. The date is that of a fall during very icy weather at Lynn, Massachusetts in which Eddy suffered a spinal injury, serious enough to have been reported in the local paper two days later[2]. Three days later, she wrote afterwards, she had 'the healing Truth' dawn upon her; Christian Scientists refer to the date of her fall as the date of the birth of their religion[3].

In the years following the fall Eddy began to charge students very considerable fees to learn her own healing technique (and additionally

---

1. Gottschalk 1973, p. 106; for Quimby's work see Dresser 1921.
2. Voorhees 2021, p. 57.
3. Eddy 1891, p. 24.

committing them to pay ten per cent of any income resulting from their knowledge), and by 1872 she had written the first 60 pages of a description of both her method and its philosophical foundations, which in 1875 was published as the first edition of her first book, entitled *Science and Health*. This self-published edition was 456 pages in length, and in its final form in 1910, after an astonishing 400-plus editions, attained 700 pages. It is in this form that the book has been published ever since that date.

Perhaps one of the reasons that there has been so little serious philosophical work on Eddy until very recently is that she was publicly hostile to the subject of philosophy as a whole, having declared it 'ninety-nine parts of error to the one-hundredth Truth'[4]. On the subdiscipline of metaphysics she wrote that 'Such miscalled metaphysical systems are reeds shaken by the wind. Compared with the inspired wisdom and infinite meaning of the Word of Truth, they are as moonbeams to the sun, or as the Stygian night is to the kindling dawn'[5].

Gottschalk[6] seems to have concluded on this basis that 'inconsistencies within her writing make a reduction of it to closed metaphysical system impossible'. However, Steiger, in his 1946 PhD thesis, 'A Philosophical Investigation of the Doctrine of Christian Science', found much of interest. Since the later work of many eminent nineteenth-century German idealists was so at odds with that of their earlier publications, while not diminishing from their reputations as philosophers, Gottschalk does seem overly harsh in this respect.

Eddy herself referred to Christian Science as a 'system', and, despite her idiosyncratic use of the word 'metaphysical' (which for the purposes of Christian Science understandably has more prominent theological overtones than is normally the case in academic philosophy), did not misrepresent her work by describing it in this way. Christian Science is a religious metaphysical system, but it is nevertheless underpinned by a thoroughgoing idealism which goes much further even than Fichte. It is Eddy's metaphysical daring in linking idealism with scientific method, and the consequences which logically follow from it, which I believe offer the opportunity for further research in this mistakenly neglected area of study.

---

4. Eddy 1887a, p. 21.
5. Eddy 1887a, p. 22.
6. 1973, p. 33.

Science and Health

Science and Health was largely written between 1872 and 1874, towards the end of a nine-year period from 1866 when Eddy had been almost entirely occupied by metaphysical matters and their relation to Christian Science. The book, from Eddy's viewpoint, was at one and the same time a textbook of Christian Science and its 'evangel'[7]. Eddy's second longest work, *Miscellaneous Writings, 1883-1896*, she later referred to as good preparatory reading for students of Christian Science before undertaking the task of reading and understanding *Science and Health*. Although Eddy regarded the ideas expressed within *Science and Health* as revealed Truth, she nevertheless had to establish a quasi-technical vocabulary for communicating these ideas. Hand in hand with the development of this technical language, which gave new and precise meanings to terms borrowed from a variety of physical sciences, medicine, theology and philosophy, came the opportunity to develop these new ideas, as the terminology permitted both a more exact expression of her existing ideas and the possibility of setting forth entirely new concepts, which would have proved difficult in the immediately preceding years owing to their sheer novelty. As Eddy explained in *Science and Health* itself[8]: 'The inadequacy of material terms for metaphysical statements' was the cause of the principal impediment in communicating the ideas of Christian Science. 'Expressing metaphysical ideas as to make them comprehensible to any reader'[9] would sometimes require hours of deliberation over a single word.

As Gottschalk[10] untactfully explained in almost clinical detail, '*Science and Health* is not written in a linear-rational style, with one idea succeeding the other in orderly progression. The statements... do not necessarily have any logical sequence, and in many cases there is no particular reason why one sentence should be placed just where it is.'

Nevertheless, no less an authority than Mark Twain described Eddy, with whose work he was very familiar, as:

> In several ways the most interesting woman who ever lived, and the most extraordinary... She has launched a world

---

7. Eddy 1913, p. 113.
8. Eddy 1910, p. 115.
9. Eddy 1910, p. 115.
10. 1973, p. 43.

> religion which now has 663 churches, and she charters a new one every four days. When we do not know a person – and when we do – we have to judge his [sic] size by the size of his [sic] achievements, as compared with the achievements of others in his [sic] special line of business – there is no other way. Measured by this standard, it is 1300 years since the world has produced anyone who could reach up to Mrs. Eddy's waistbelt.[11]

Notwithstanding, he considered *Science and Health* 'Strange and frantic and incomprehensible and uninterpretable', descriptions which may have been influenced by tensions within his own family: his own daughter Clara Clemens not only joined the Christian Scientist Church, but ultimately wrote a book on the subject[12].

Thomas[13] suggested that Eddy's ideas could have, at the very least, been influenced by the American transcendentalists, who had amongst their numbers many respected authors, such as Emerson and Thoreau, and that in Eddy's case, of particular importance was Bronson Alcott, the father of Louisa May Alcott (author of *Little Women*, and as a result the funder of her father's work). A further source for some of her central ideas both quoted and acknowledged in *Science and Health* from the 24th to the 33rd editions, is Vedanta philosophy. Ideas from the Upanishads indirectly asserting the unreality of both suffering and the material universe were employed[14], though from approximately 1885 Eddy sought to emphasise the differences between Hinduism (and other Eastern religions) and Christian Science; *Science and Health* from the 34th edition onwards no longer contained either the quotes or any references to Eastern religions.

W.F. Evans (a Swedenborgian minister and healer who along with Eddy studied under Quimby and who was an already well-established author when Eddy launched her Christian Science) had written extensively on the action of the mind in relation to illness, and was well versed in both theology and metaphysical philosophy, making him aware of the potential links between 'mind-cures' and Hegelian and Fichtean idealism, as well as the philosophy within Hinduism

---

11. Twain 1907, pp. 102-103.
12. Clemens 1956.
13. 1930.
14. Farnsworth 1909, p. 5.

and Buddhism. To what extent, if any, Evans' work influenced Eddy is hard to assess with any accuracy, but whatever the truth, Eddy was far more radical and her system of thought in many ways the opposite of Evans': he believed matter to be perfect, whereas Eddy denied its existence; Evans held desire to be the key to self-realisation, but Eddy considered the eradication of desire to be essential (Gill 1998, p. 313).

There are clearly areas of commonality between the American transcendentalists of mid-nineteenth-century New England and the ideas foundational to Eddy's Christian Science, developed a few decades later. American transcendentalism evolved from a merging of concepts from German romanticism and idealism of the years either side of 1800, albeit as interpreted by British authors. Alcott was initially very impressed with the first edition of *Science and Health* in 1875, seeing it as an important new development in the resistance against philosophical materialism. However, in 1878, after what would be his last meeting with Eddy, it was her sheer radicalism which unsettled him, and he later wrote that there 'is perhaps a touch of fanaticism, though of genial quality, interposed into her faith'[15]; given Eddy's extraordinary degree of financial success and considerable oeuvre of published work, he may well have been correct.

Emerson, originally perhaps the most radically idealist of the transcendentalists, had by the 1870s backtracked on the position he had previously expressed in *Nature*[16]. Eddy, therefore, was not only more extreme in her idealism, but also moving in the opposite direction to the by then ageing transcendentalists. It can be argued that she was more consistent than they had been, in that she accepted the logical consequences of idealism, rather than balking at the counterintuitive implications.

The content and structure of the text

This book demonstrates the following aspects of Eddy's thought:

1. There are two components to Eddy's metaphysics: the aprioristic and the empirical. Her application of what is arguably scientific method (although one may dispute the choice of her experimental data, which ignores cases in

---

15. Shepherd 1938, p. 489.
16. Emerson 1836, pp. 1-4.

which 'healings' have not occurred) creates what might be termed 'applied metaphysics'.
2. There is coherence in her thinking and a commitment to accept some highly counterintuitive consequences arising from it; this is particularly the hallmark of a philosopher.
3. Her claims and her method of arriving at them correspond to those of earlier and later academic philosophers.
4. Although her system of thought leads to objections that she may not be able to counter, this does not imply that no coherent philosophical argument is present. Many idealist philosophers can be refuted, and within general philosophy virtually all of the conclusions of the still-studied, highly respected Presocratic philosophers are no longer accepted without this affecting their status as philosophers.

The subsequent chapters are as follows.

Chapter 2 Christian Science and Eddy's idealism

Distilled from the million-or-so words of Eddy's writing, this chapter begins the summarising of her philosophical system, its context and its interconnections, and presents an outline of Eddy's work, providing sufficient depth and breadth to indicate the possibility of reframing the conceptual core of her magnum opus, *Science and Health*, as idealist philosophy. I also briefly discuss the only two PhDs which appear ever to have been written regarding the philosophical basis of her work.

Chapter 3 Eddy from near and far

This chapter considers the contributions made to Eddy's system of thought by Evans and Quimby and their ideas. Initially sharing a set of questions relating to mind, matter and gender, Eddy ultimately diverged from these and other major figures. Recent important biographical studies are also referred to, providing a counterbalancing element of twenty-first-century thought. After a detailed synopsis of its contents, I will establish a minimal representative subset, and then restructure and rephrase the text so as to reduce the redundancy (due to considerable repetition) and ambiguity (due to imprecise language) present in the original.

Chapter 4 Robert Peel and the conceptual bridge

The work of Robert Peel provides the conceptual bridge between Eddy's philosophical system and its application as a form of healing. A lifelong Christian Scientist himself, Peel could see both sides of this divide in his daily life. His three-volume biography of Eddy is by far the longest and most detailed of any written so far, and the many healings of which he had direct experience led him to pursue analytically the challenge Christian Science clearly presents to a conventional understanding of the physical sciences, such as physics, chemistry and biology.

Chapter 5 The philosophical analysis of Christian Science

A multiplicity of relevant general texts exist concerning idealism which are of obvious use in assisting with the identification of idealism in Mary Baker Eddy's writing. Narrowing the remit concerning these general texts on idealism is essential, as the field is far too large to conveniently survey and only certain types of idealism are helpful for this analysis.

In order to represent it clearly, this chapter contains a minimal subset of the 'propositions' at the heart of Eddy's system, and corollaries which follow from them, leading to an exhaustive comparison of each of the possible pairings of the elements from this subset, testing every possible pairing of propositions for consistency.

Chapter 6 Christian Science as a philosophical system

This chapter is a philosophical exploration of the restructured and rephrased expression of the ideas present in *Science and Health*. It demonstrates the radical idealism upon which the work is based, and identifies and makes explicit the subtly different forms of idealism which are present. Following on from the presentation of Eddy's system in a concise form, this chapter contains a higher-level analysis of her work, identifying and then focussing particularly on a number of possible problems which, if unresolved, could entirely demolish her intellectual edifice. In brief, these are:

1. Her occasional use of seemingly antithetical physicalist/materialist language and the concepts to which it relates;
2. Her use and understanding of the word 'everything'; and

3. The fundamental difficulty concerning the human 'error' of misperception, the possibility of which being absolutely essential to her system.

I offer potential solutions to these difficulties, which in at least one case may be entirely new.

Chapter 7 Christian Science reframed

This chapter begins to consider apparently paradoxical elements of Eddy's thought, before focussing on a narrow set of critical difficulties.

Chapter 8 Eddy's radicalism: Problems and solutions

Several themes result from the analysis in the previous chapters. They include strikingly original contributions made by Eddy to the philosophy of religion, facets of her belief system characterisable as the limiting case of idealism, and the entire methodology of 'empirical metaphysics', but also a number of ambiguities and potentially paradoxical statements. This chapter therefore focusses on these difficulties and provides potential solutions to them.

Chapter 9 Criticism and controversy: The Spanish Influenza and the COVID-19 pandemic

Given the Christian Science position regarding the nonexistence of illness, this chapter contains understandably polemic material diametrically at odds with established science and medicine, but stresses the many reasons why conflating Eddy's position regarding illness and that of 'COVID deniers' would represent a new injustice.

Chapter 10 Conclusions and suggestions for further research

This chapter presents the results of the analysis in a summarised form and make a number of suggestions for further research. A recapitulation of particular similarities between Eddy's conclusions and those later published by the British idealist philosopher John McTaggart forms part of the chapter, demonstrating that, despite following completely different lines of argument, both Eddy and

McTaggart agree that the ultimate, 'highest' form of entity within the radically idealist universe they both asserted, subsuming all others, is Love.

Bibliography

The detailed bibliography contains references from a great variety of useful sources, despite the historic lack of research in the philosophy of this subject.

Glossary of terms

Eddy's work introduces a large number of specialist terms, and redefines existing terms from theology and other disciplines with sometimes entirely different meanings to the original. Although this will be explained where necessary throughout the book, for clarity a thorough glossary will also be provided.

The author's involvement

My first contact with the work of Mary Baker Eddy was while carrying out background reading for the dissertation component of an MA in Philosophy with the UK's Open University. I had become very interested in pacifism in general (and absolute pacifism in particular) and, while investigating the different reasons which religious groups offered as justification for the most extreme form of pacifism, I was astounded to discover that, during World War 2, at least some Christian Scientists, when asked how and why God could permit such slaughter, replied that it was obvious that it couldn't be happening, and must therefore be an illusion[17]. Fascinated, I started to explore the defining texts of Christian Science, and discovered that its founder, Mary Baker Eddy, had created a theology underpinned by the most thoroughgoing form of idealism which I had ever met.

Partially obscured by her occasionally nebulous style, I felt, was evidence of an idealist philosopher of great depth, breadth and originality, yet on searching for academic analyses of her work, only two names appeared with any frequency. Why had her work been so neglected by academia? The charge of nebulousness, and, at times, a

---

17. Wilcox 1941, p. 2.

certain lack of logical progression in her arguments could be brought against many well-known idealist philosophers of the nineteenth century. My hypothesis is that the neglect is at least in part due to her gender.

It is time for a reassessment of her work. In recent years there has been an upsurge of interest in previously overlooked female philosophers from throughout history[18]. Mary Baker Eddy's work fits into this category, with the injustice in her case being twofold, in that her work has not merely been largely ignored by the academic community, but is also not recognised even as coherent philosophy, let alone highly original coherent philosophy.

The first stage necessary is to begin the endeavour and privilege of presenting and analysing Eddy's system of thought, known as Christian Science, in a clear and logically sequenced form. No analysis is performed, however, as this takes place in later chapters following the re-expression of Eddy's ideas.

The overall approach can be thought of as the extraction, re-expression and analysis of Mary Baker Eddy's key ideas and core concepts from her published works, which I refer to as the 'gold'. As with actual gold mining, there is a very great deal of material surrounding the gold which has to be removed; in the case of Mary Baker Eddy it is the ornamentation, ambiguity and repetitiveness of her prose which dilutes the gold of her ideas.

A further aspect of Mary Baker Eddy's work which I believe has led to its misidentification as fringe theology, rather than core philosophy, is that her use of language, even when stripped of the above-mentioned redundancy, is that of a layperson untutored in academic philosophy. This, combined with her idiosyncratic redefinitions of existing technical terms from theology (and also her demotic language) creates a further barrier preventing her recognition as a highly original and thoroughgoing idealist philosopher.

Setting the 'gold' in context

Before exploring Mary Baker Eddy's idealism in detail, it is useful to establish where her ideas place her in the spectrum of different forms of idealism, and in what ways her concepts are similar to, or different from, the thought of well-known idealist philosophers. Placing

---

18. Thomas 2018, p. 1.

her ideas in context, of course, requires a summary of her work sufficiently detailed for this purpose yet concise enough not to be unwieldy. Luckily, Mary Baker Eddy herself provided a precis which can form the basis of this summary in Chapter 14 of her work, *Science and Health*[19], and Steiger concludes with a similar conspectus in the last chapter of his 1946 PhD thesis[20].

At their centre, Mary Baker Eddy's ideas are breathtakingly radical: like Fichte she rejects the existence of the thing-in-itself[21], but, far beyond this, counters the Cartesian view that sensory experience, even with regard to pain and emotional states, is not a separate category to cognition. It is important to stress at the outset that this goes beyond Berkeleyan idealism; what Eddy is asserting is, for example, that *an individual can be mistaken about believing themselves to be in pain*. This claim is only coherent if one accepts (for the purpose of argument) the concept that the experience of pain is actually a belief, that beliefs are the result of cognition, and that cognition can lead to error. From Eddy's standpoint, an individual who expresses the belief that they are in pain is simply wrong, and by correcting this false belief, the imagined, unreal pain will cease. In this particular case Eddy would be entirely certain, even without examining the supposed cause, as her theology (which is ultimately the result of deductive argument rather than mere conjecture or an assertion of faith), denies the existence of pain.

Once the overly ornamental and repetitive language has been removed, the next task is to re-express Eddy's core ideas in the language of academic philosophy. This will make the concepts involved clearer and permit the demonstration of the coherency of the arguments she put forward for her beliefs.

There are many components to Eddy's idealism, some being recognisable as similar to the concepts of Fichte and von Hardenberg (who wrote under the pseudonym 'Novalis'), others as similar to those of Hegel and Schopenhauer, but, most importantly, a further set as similar to those of the later British idealists, and particularly to McTaggart. In some cases, Eddy's work predated the publication of these ideas in academic literature by as much as 50 years, as is true with the second volume of McTaggart's *The Nature of Existence*.

---

19. Eddy 1910, pp. 465 ff.
20. Steiger 1946, pp. 272-85.
21. Fichte (1987 [1800]) 1994 [1797], pp. 12-16.

It is also important to point out certain contrasts between Eddy's system of thought and those of well-known idealists, and, even more importantly, between Eddy's metaphysical system and how it can be easily misinterpreted. The most commonly held misunderstanding regarding Christian Science is that it is either 'faith healing' or a 'mind cure'. Although I have already touched upon this issue, it so crucial to what follows that I will make mention of it throughout the text as it becomes relevant at each point. Fundamental to Christian Science theology is that *illness does not exist*; what happens (adherents claim) when an individual's symptoms disappear as a result of the process undertaken by Christian Science practitioners is that the patient *realises the truth of this fact*.

Moving on

Although this book relates solely to the philosophy underlying Christian Science, the fact that this has hitherto been little researched necessitates trawling for relevant philosophical content in a variety of atypical sources, the identities of which are sometimes quite counterintuitive. Apart from a very few texts specifically on the idealism in Eddy's work, these other sources fall into five principal categories:

1. Biographies of Eddy with philosophical content;
2. Theological texts on Christian Science, but explaining at least some of the idealism upon which it is founded;
3. Works highly critical of Christian Science (and some of Eddy personally), which in seeking to argue against her system of thought, provide a useful exposition of the philosophy in question;
4. Works of fiction which are in reality simply vehicles for the author to express their enthusiasm for Christian Science, and in seeking to justify it against its critics, offer detailed philosophical arguments for its validity; and
5. Works making specific though false accusations regarding Eddy or Christian Science, but which apart from obvious falsehoods nevertheless address 'Eddy's challenge to materialism'[22].

---

22. Gottschalk 2006, p. v.

The last three categories, and especially the last of all, are perhaps surprising at first sight, but taking the fifth category as an example, there are excellent historical precedents for this eclectic approach. Tocqueville's *Democracy in America* is an exemplar[23] written following his extended investigative voyage around America, it notoriously contained many serious errors and misunderstandings, yet was critically acclaimed as being the best book on democracy in the USA up until that date, because the errors lay outside its purpose and focus. Assessed as an analysis of America's implementation of democracy, it was unrivalled, despite the erroneous content.

---

23. Tocqueville 1835, 1840.

Chapter 2

Christian Science and Eddy's Metaphysical Idealism

Distilled from the million-or-so words Eddy used to describe her system of thought, this chapter summarises Eddy's philosophical ideas and their interconnections.

As with all religions, Christian Science is defined by its particular set of beliefs and practices, which in this case are part of the metaphysical family of religious movements. In addition to the Bible, it has another book which is considered an inspired text: *Science and Health* (1910), the principal work of its founder and in which the main tenets are explained. Eddy wrote over a dozen other books addressing specific issues: *Manual of the Mother Church* (1895); *Miscellaneous Writings* (1897); *Retrospection and Introspection* (1891); *Unity of Good* (1888); *Pulpit and Press* (1895); *Rudimental Divine Science* (1887); *No and Yes* (1887); *Christian Science versus Pantheism* (1898); *Message to the Mother Church, 1900* (1900); *Message to the Mother Church, 1901* (1901); *Message to the Mother Church, 1902* (1902); *Christian Healing* (1886); *The People's Idea of God* (1883); *Poems* (1910); *Christ and Christmas* (Eddy and Gilman 1894); and *The First Church of Christ, Scientist and Miscellany* (1913. I list these here to illustrate the breadth and depth of Eddy's work and, so as to further emphasise this point, it may be necessary for readers outside the USA to learn that in a poll of the *most influential Americans of all time*, i.e. in any field of endeavour, not 'just' religion, she was included in the top

100[1]. Her degree of importance is not in doubt; it is the nature of that importance I address.

As mentioned earlier, amongst the most important of Christian Science beliefs is the idea that illness is an illusion (which can be corrected, not cured, as it does not exist, only by prayer), but even more critical to the later analysis is the Christian Science assertion that this fact is simply a consequence of the entirety of material reality being illusory.

Mary Baker Eddy as an idealist philosopher

Idealism in all of its various forms – subjective, objective, absolute, magical, personal and many less well-known other types – rejects the physicalist (materialist) notion that ultimate reality consists of the entities familiar to 'common-sense', naïve models of the universe, i.e. that our awareness of objects is as they actually are, and that they are composed of matter, occupy space and obey the laws of physics, including those which relate to the categories of energy, space and time[2]. Instead, it regards its ultimate constituents as non-material entities; for example, love and souls[3]. Eddy's world view thus fits precisely within this paradigm, in that she too rejected the physicalist concepts in favour of these idealist forms. Fundamentally, by denying the supposed evidence of our senses, and recasting them as false cognitions, Eddy was able to redefine the common-sense understanding of reality described earlier as 'error'[4].

Idealists fall into one or other of two categories, either being descriptive or revisionist metaphysicians, with the former group rejecting the materialist epistemological understanding of the nature of reality[5] and the latter group denying the materialist ontological model of reality[6]. This categorisation is entirely sufficient for the purposes of this chapter, but acknowledged as being simplistic and arguably incomplete.

---

1. *The Atlantic Monthly*, December 2006.
2. Putnam 2012, pp. 39-50.
3. McTaggart 1927, p. 156.
4. Eddy 1910, p. 13.
5. e.g. Berkeley 1710, §§XVII-XXI.
6. e.g. Fichte 1800 in the Preuss translation 1987, p. 104.

Eddy, although superficially a Fichtean, went much further, rejecting the nature of Kant's things-in-themselves and all the apparent evidence of our senses, replacing them with an alternative set which she believed to be grasped by an innate, spiritual sense and to which she was convinced that individuals could be awakened by the methods of her Church, officially referred to as The First Church of Christ, Scientist[7].

Many of the early critics of Christian Science appreciated that the conceptual framework at the centre of Eddy's work was a very much more radical form of idealism than had been previously espoused. For example, Wolcott pointed out that Berkeley 'never reduces idealism to absurdity attempting to apply it to the affairs of everyday life, and the conclusions of universal experience'[8]. Berkeley, of course, in explaining his own form of idealism had stated that 'I do not argue against the existence of any one thing that we can comprehend either of sensation or reflection; that the things I see with my eyes and touch with my hands do exist, I make not the slightest question. The only thing whose existence I do deny is that which philosophers call matter or corporeal substance'[9].

Eddy, however, denied exactly the component of reality which Berkeley so explicitly left untouched, and equally explicitly made this distinction between herself and Berkeley entirely clear[10]. Also, she states: 'that by knowing the unreality of disease, sin and death, you demonstrate the allness [sic] of God'[11]. This assertion was made on the basis that 'As human thought changes from one stage to another of conscious pain and painlessness, sorrow and joy, – from fear to hope and from faith to understanding, – the visible manifestation will at last be man governed by Soul, not by material sense'[12].

Eddy's radical ideas resulted from a very lengthy search for a successful treatment for her many and varied health difficulties. In 1861 Eddy discovered the method created by Phineas Quimby, who had developed his techniques for healing after abruptly recovering

---

7. Stark 1998, p. 193.
8. Wolcott 1896, p. 15.
9. Berkeley quoted in Buckley 1901, p. 23.
10. Eddy 1901, pp. 23-24.
11. Eddy 1887, p. 9, 10.
12. Eddy 1910, p .125.

from what had been diagnosed as tuberculosis[13]. Quimby's approach was initially based on mesmerism, the nineteenth-century term for a form of hypnosis, after Franz Mesmer. Mesmer had been working at a time when magnetic and electrical phenomena were being scientifically investigated for the first time and were a fashionable interest for many leading figures in European and American society. Influenced by the zeitgeist, Mesmer had interpreted his genuinely impressive results as being due to a hypothetical magnetic fluid permitting living things to affect one another by a process which Mesmer termed 'animal magnetism'[14]. Quimby, however, working several decades later in 1847, when electrical phenomena were becoming better understood, considered that the effect of suggestion, rather than any magnetic or electrical process, was responsible for the occasional cures he was achieving. Having determined that neither a hypothetical 'fluid' nor 'animal magnetism' was involved in the process, he instead considered that illness was in reality a state of mind – a perfectly reasonable deduction given that the 'cures' appeared to be resulting from suggestion.

Quimby also found theological justification: the well-known Biblical account in which Christ heals a paralysed man, was, Quimby claimed, an example of something similar. He explained it as follows: 'There is no intelligence, no power or action in matter of itself... the spiritual world to which our eyes are closed by ignorance or unbelief is the real world... in it lie all the causes for every visible effect in the natural world.'[15] Quimby's method, therefore, was to explain to the patient that their own mind could control their symptoms.

The influence which Quimby had on Eddy's direction of thought was considerable, but despite his genuine success with his own professional activities as a healer, he was a largely uneducated man who knew nothing of the idealists. Eddy's subsequent contact with the Methodist minister Warren Felt Evans was very different in nature, however. Evans had read widely on metaphysical philosophy and theology, and was well aware of the connection between his ideas regarding the effect of the mind, the work of Fichte, Hegel and Edwards, and the various philosophies underpinning Eastern

---

13. Dresser 1921, pp. 28, 29.
14. Mesmer 1779, in the 1948 translation p. 31.
15. Quimby quoted in Dresser 1921, pp. 319-20.

religions such as Hinduism and Buddhism, eventually arriving at Swedenborgianism[16].

Of the German idealists, Fichte comes closest to providing a formal framework for much of Eddy's ideas, notably in *The Vocation of Man*[17].

The use of the word 'science'

In the 1870s, at the time Eddy wrote *Science and Health*, the physical sciences were already beginning to be seen as the reference standard for claims regarding knowledge. A modern critic of Christian Science, therefore, might reasonably suppose that Eddy chose to use the word 'science' in the name for her new discipline simply to gain it extra authority and increase its standing among the general public, but this would be to do Eddy a great disservice. From her point of view, Christian Science was exactly what she claimed of it – a science – not just in the Aristotelian sense of knowledge in general, and certainly not in the pseudoscientific sense in which the word is sometimes now misappropriated, but in precisely the way that the word had become used by the rapidly advancing sciences of physics and chemistry, yet applied to a different 'data set': it offered claims which were testable, yet related to a metaphysical rather than mechanistic reality.

This genuine commitment to the true principle of science explains the very considerable antipathy which Eddy felt for mysticism and mind cures, with which she was sometimes wrongly conflated, and from which she believed her philosophy to be wholly separate. Prayer, for Eddy, was 'an act'[18] within a spiritual universe, and the change in experience thus resulting was evidence – scientific evidence – for its effectiveness.

Although the mechanistic understanding of our experiences of the hypothetical 'physical reality' is now almost universal, it is nevertheless a theoretical construct. Assembling a set of (assumed-to-be) sense perceptions into a unified whole is a purely mental abstraction, in which we posit the existence of solid objects in an objective, external universe with causality as its foundational principle. Developments in the 1920s in the field of quantum physics

---

16. Evans 1869, pp. 220, 221.
17. Fichte 1987.
18. Gottschalk 1973, p. 281.

have provided extra evidence (extra to that of Hinduism, Jainism, Buddhism and Sikhism, that is) that a naïve realism (realism here being used in the philosophical sense, i.e. the opposite of philosophical idealism) is far from an accurate representation of reality. Einstein showed that physical measurements such as velocity and distance are subjective, depending on the frame of reference of the observer[19], and even causality is an illusion created by the statistics central to the uncertainty principle[20]. As Bradley put it:

> To speak generally, the mechanical view [i.e. mechanistic] is non-sense [sic], because the position of the laws is quite inconsistent and unintelligible. This is a defect which belongs to every special science... but in the sphere of Nature reaches its lowest extreme... since these laws are not physical, and since on the other hand they seem essential to Nature, the essence of Nature seems, therefore, to be made alien to itself.[21]

The point which Bradley is making here is that a nineteenth-century physicist would assert that only matter and energy exist, yet the laws of physics are neither, thus immediately demonstrating that something non-physical has to exist even in a pre-Einsteinian, naïvely mechanistic universe model. In the literal definition of 'metaphysics' – from the Greek μετά (meta, meaning 'after' or 'beyond') – the laws of physics would appear to fit rather well, and somewhat counterintuitively could themselves be seen as representing a first step into a larger world.

Eddy's historic misrepresentation

Another facet in the complex set of reasons which have prevented Eddy from being fully recognised as an idealist philosopher so far is her claim, variously and repeatedly expressed, that her principal work, *Science and Health* was an 'inspired book'[22]. Having previously disparaged 99 per cent of the academic philosophy that might have

---

19. Einstein 1920.
20. Heisenberg 1927.
21. Bradley 1893, p. 354.
22. Gottschalk 1973, p. xxi.

been thought to underpin her magnum opus, now she *appeared* to be additionally removing herself from its authorship. This is just one of the many reasons why her work has not been perceived as philosophy, others being documented later.

The complexity of Eddy's historic misrepresentation is sufficient to warrant a small taxonomy in its own right. The main reasons for this century-long injustice appear to fall into the following broad categories:

1. Sexist prejudice: self-evidently still present in the twenty-first century, but far worse in the nineteenth and twentieth centuries;
2. The theological prominence of Christian Science outshining the philosophical content upon which it is based;
3. The politics of envy: Eddy's great financial success;
4. Inappropriateness of status: Eddy held no degrees or appointments outside of the institution which she had created;
5. Linguistic inexpertise: Eddy's ideas ran beyond her ability to express them;
6. Outlandishness: the sheer originality and extreme nature of the philosophy underpinning Christian Science creates a barrier between critics and a genuine attempt to engage with its ideas;
7. Offensiveness: conservatively minded clerics were genuinely offended by some of Eddy's redefinitions and reinterpretations, e.g. regarding the nature of the Trinity and Christ's purpose on earth; and
8. Eddy's notoriety as a public figure, caused by (but independent of) the fame engendered by her role as the 'discoverer' of Christian Science (e.g. "In the year 1866, I discovered the Christ Science")[23]), creating an identity far from that stereotypically expected of a philosopher.

Some of these reasons are evident from the contemporary and extensive published criticism of Eddy and Christian Science, some are inferences from Eddy's own writing, and the remainder are prima facie conjectures.

---

23. Eddy 1910, p. 107.

The idea

Mary Baker Eddy's argument, in a paraphrased form, is roughly as follows. In this promulgation I will initially treat Eddy's assumption that God exists as axiomatic of her metaphysical system, but this is temporary, and only for the purpose of launching her argument; it will be replaced later with what she regarded as experimental proof for God's existence. Beginning with an observation initially not unlike that of Berkeley, she notes that only minds can have ideas, and concurs that physical matter cannot be responsible for mental function, on the basis that mere matter cannot possess the ideas processed by cognition; for cognition to be able to access these ideas, it must be composed of the same immaterial substance that Eddy considered must be responsible for these ideas; both aspects of mental function must therefore be incorporeal[24]. Although Eddy arrived at this independently, it is essentially a Fichtean position, and not original in itself, but she immediately goes further with her argument in a way which I believe is original. By reassessing what we refer to as our senses as instead creating not sensation but false beliefs, she is able to create the possibility that all 'sensory' experience can be subject to error, ending what was then two centuries of acceptance of the Cartesian idea that sensory experiences are incorrigible[25]

The consequences

Eddy's argument permits a complete reassessment of what we believe ourselves to be and what we imagine ourselves to exist within. Without hyperbole, it is hard to conceive of any element of what one might have assumed to be the case about our universe, life and God that is not, in principle at least, modified by her argument. It is worthwhile recapping at this point exactly what Eddy was claiming, and also taking the opportunity to add a little more detail. Of great importance in the terminology specific to Christian Science is the word 'error'. In Christian Science, it has an ontological aspect which can be negated by divine Truth; error, therefore, ceases to exist once this Truth has been realised. Eddy held that any belief system which posited the reality or power of anything other than God is in error;

---

24. Eddy 1910, p. 335.
25. Raff 1966, pp.595-637.

one of the consequences of this idea is that the concept of evil is itself an example of human-generated error.

The classical explanation for the existence of evil offered by conventional Christian theology is that freedom of will created the freedom to sin, with evil being the result. Eddy's solution to the age-old 'problem of evil' (known in academic theology as 'theodicy') was as breathtakingly simple as it was astoundingly radical: evil does not exist.

Unusually for a religion, both then and now, Christian Science strongly rejects any form of mysticism, with instead a declared preference for science and scientific method. Despite its profoundly metaphysical basis, Eddy saw her discovery as part of empirical science; 'empirical metaphysics' might summarise her discovery. This is a very substantive claim, and therefore requires a careful and thorough justification. How are the methods of science to be reconciled with Eddy's claim? Does this mean that she thinks that the ontology of natural science, i.e. matter, can be separated from its methodology, i.e. the empirical method?

Perhaps surprisingly, the answer is a resounding 'yes'. Eddy believed that the healings she and her disciples achieved (whatever we may believe to be the actual reason for them) were empirical confirmation for her foundational belief, namely that illness is an illusion. The observable, repeatable fact of the (occasional yet genuine) 'cures' served exactly the function of an experiment in any of the physical sciences, not proving a hypothesis but providing evidence that it *may* be true. If Eddy had never achieved any healings, then her hypothesis would have been contradicted, as it fulfils the criteria for a scientific hypothesis: it can be falsified.

Although Christian Science is best known for these controversial claims regarding illness, this aspect is both greatly misunderstood by the general public and a corollary of a belief system, rather than a core belief itself; it can be thought of as 'applied' idealism, very much in line with the suggestion made by von Hardenberg (who wrote under the pseudonym 'Novalis') in the 1790s within what he termed 'magical idealism' (explained later). The healing performed by Christian Science practitioners involves helping the patient to deny the existence of their illness, wholly unlike faith-based healing claimed by evangelical Churches on the right wing of mainstream Christianity. The profoundly radical idealism of Christian Science is therefore not confined to abstract, philosophical analysis and discussion, fascinating though this naturally is; Eddy, like the British idealist McTaggart a few decades later, asserted that the 'Love that is God'[26] is the one, true reality, and that 'frighteningly real' (ibid.) suffering and illness are in truth 'waking dream-shadows'[27]. By ceasing to make the error of mistaking the false evidence of our senses for reality, 'we draw closer to God'[28] and suffering is reduced or eliminated according to the degree of a particular individual's realisation of this unreality.

Regarding the widely assumed incorrigibility of the knowledge of mental states gained by introspection, it *has* been questioned in academic philosophy, but rarely. One example is from D.M. Armstrong, and it appeared 88 years after the publication of *Science and Health*:

> The apprehension of something must be distinct from the thing apprehended. For, if not, we are faced with a flagrant circularity. Having a pain logically involves the apprehension of – what? The pain itself! This is as bad as saying that to be a cat logically involves being the offspring of cats.[29]

Armstrong here offers us the possibility that the 'thing apprehended' is the error; the apprehension can therefore vanish.

On the basis that illness and death are consequences of the false belief in the existence of evil, the corollary is therefore that these are also unreal: 'We bow down to matter and entertain finite thoughts of God like the pagan idolater. Mortals are inclined to fear and obey what they consider a material body more than they do a spiritual God.'[30]

Eddy's position could therefore be seen as being more consistent than Berkeley, in that she accepts the logical implication of her commitment to the belief in God as an immaterial being, whereas Berkeley can be seen as backing away from what should be his conclusions. Berkeley's 'immaterialism', now referred to as subjective idealism, is predicated upon the idea that we can only perceive

---

26. Gottschalk 2006, p. 83.
27. Eddy 1910, p. 418.
28. Gottschalk 2006, p. 83.
29. Armstrong 1963, p. 423.
30. Eddy 1910, p. 214.

sensations, as opposed to externalities, which have to be perceived in order to exist. What Berkeley backed away from is the logical consequence of this understanding of reality, which, somewhat ironically, was best expressed by G.E. Moore in his 1903 paper, 'The Refutation of Idealism'[31]. He argued that for Berkeley to be correct, object and subject would have to be necessarily connected such that there cannot be any distinction between an object and its perception. Berkeley, however, although asserting that we cannot directly know external objects (with only sense perceptions being available to us), did not advance the model of reality in which these sense perceptions are the reality in question.

Crucial to Eddy's extension of this idea is her replacement of 'material senses', which she argued were simply false beliefs, with 'spiritual sense', which, as part of divine thought, is both the direct perception of reality and reality itself. Eddy's thoroughgoing idealism also had consequences for the nature of the human body, in that she denied the existence of a material body, instead asserting the sole existence of Spirit. It might be thought – wrongly, in my view – that these ultimately amount to the same thing. Although Berkeley asserted that what exists is ideal, which entails a denial of the existence of matter on the ground that ideas of mind-independent material things could not even be conceived, Berkeley was only denying the nature of what appear to be material objects, never the fact of their existence; he would not, for example, deny the reality of illness.

It is also worth emphasising another extreme claim of Christian Science and particularly its consequence: as God is the Principle (to use Eddy's preferred term) of all reality, the real nature of the universe and of man is divine perfection; the universe and man are spiritual, eternal and – crucially – perfect. 'All is infinite Mind and its infinite manifestation', Eddy wrote[32], referring to the nature of existence as 'ideas'. 'Metaphysics resolves things into thoughts, and exchanges the objects of sense for the ideas of the Soul'[33]. Another fascinating example of Eddy's ingenuity regarding the manipulation of ideas follows from this observation. Having determined that, as part of the Divine, man is perfect, Eddy deduces that nearly two millennia of theological exegesis had entirely failed to understand Scripture at

---

31. Moore 1903.
32. 1910, p. 246.
33. Eddy, 1910, p. 269.

Matthew v. 48: 'Be ye therefore perfect, even as your Father which is in heaven is perfect' (KJV). Far from that being an entreatment to attempt to gain or aspire to perfection, Jesus was explaining to his audience that *mankind is already perfect*.

As God is infinitely good and God is everything, man is in reality part of the divine consciousness and therefore perfect. Man, therefore, cannot sin; sin and evil are the consequence of an error of belief, as they are unreal. Christ, it follows, did not come to save mankind from sin, but to save us from the *belief in sin*[34]. The nonexistence of sin necessarily changes the meaning of hell, which becomes the suffering resulting from errors such as the belief in sin and death.

Criticisms of Eddy's ideas and her own responses to them

Eddy's fame, both for her controversial ideas and for her considerable financial acumen, encouraged a range of critics, including theologians, clergymen, physicians and other people as prominent as Eddy in public life. It is the subject of some of these criticisms to which the focus now moves, as this provides further opportunities to distinguish her subtle ideas from the crude misrepresentations of her critics.

Christian Science was vigorously attacked in the late nineteenth century by both the Roman Catholic Church and the Protestant Churches which were so prominent a part of life in the New England of Eddy's era. Having previously had to deal with Berkeleyan idealism a century-and-a-half before, and the American transcendentalists 50 years in the past, now the established Churches faced a very much more extreme form of idealism. Whereas neither Berkeley nor Emerson had denied the existence of common-sense ontology, simply seeking to reinterpret its nature, Eddy denied corporeal existence entirely, going beyond the 'mere' assertion of the nonexistence of pain, illness and death. This they found extremely threatening, as absolutely central to their concept of Christ was His dual nature of being at one and the same time fully human and fully God; fully human in conventional theological terms required the possession of a corporeal body.

---

34. Eddy 1910, pp. 38, 289, 430 and 497.

Evangelical Churches also have Christ's corporeal resurrection as a central tenet, and some also have the belief that His Second Coming will be in corporeal form; many usually rather separate branches of Christianity therefore found themselves united against Christian Science. An often-made accusation was that, having borrowed its foundational principles from Hinduism, it was therefore pantheistic[35]. This mistaken assumption became so widespread that eventually, in 1898, Eddy wrote and published *Christian Science versus Pantheism*, in which she emphasised the unity and infinity of God, but absolutely refuted the idea that He/She 'dwells' within material objects.

Christian Science, despite the accusations of Eddy's critics over the last 145 years, is not pantheistic. In contrast, even the Trinity doctrine as understood by mainstream Churches concerned Eddy as being polytheistic; Christian Scientists regard God as the 'divine Principle' and 'incorporeal, divine, principle, supreme, life, truth, love'. Regarding Jesus, Christian Science considers the divine conception as being of a spiritual being, and that 'Jesus' and 'Christ' are not precisely synonymous. Instead, Jesus is taken to refer to the man, and Christ to the 'divine idea', owing to the logical consequence of the belief that good cannot dwell within an (illusory) physical body. As Eddy explains 'The Christ is incorporeal, spiritual'[36] and additionally 'matter is mortal error... matter is unreal and temporal'[37]. Combining these concepts leads to the corollary that the apparent humanity of Jesus was illusory, 'as it seemed to mortal view'[38].

Eddy's conception of the Holy Spirit is particularly original, and breathtakingly presumptuous: Christian Science *is* the Holy Spirit. Explaining this profoundly counterintuitive viewpoint, and using her preferred term, Holy Ghost, she stated that: 'The advent of this understanding is what is meant by the descent of the Holy Ghost, - that influx of divine Science which so illuminated the Pentecostal Day and is now repeating its ancient history'[39]. Eddy saw Christian Science as a *process* as well as a body of knowledge, defining her divine Science as the development of Life, Truth and Love[40], and

---

35. e.g. McCorkle 1899, p. 7.
36. Eddy 1910, p. 332.
37. Eddy 1897, p. 21.
38. Eddy 1910, p. 315.
39. Eddy 1910, p. 43.
40. Eddy 1910, p. 43.

referred to Scripture as further evidence in support of the exegesis above: '[Jesus'] students then received the Holy Ghost. By this is meant that by all they had witnessed and suffered, they were roused to an enlarged understanding of divine Science'[41].

The most explicit example of this belief is from the chapter of *Science and Health* entitled 'Apocalypse': 'John saw in those days the spiritual idea as the Messiah, who would baptize with the Holy Ghost, – divine Science'[42]. Given that mainstream Christianity adheres to the Scriptural principle that there can be no forgiveness for blasphemy against the Holy Spirit, this particular claim of Christian Science created a permanent rift between it and other forms of Christianity.

Many Christian denominations share this belief regarding blasphemy against the Holy Spirit, which follows from a number of explicit statements on the issue throughout the New Testament and their subsequent exegesis. For example:

> Wherefore I say unto you, All manner of sin and blasphemy shall be forgiven unto men: but the blasphemy against the Holy Ghost shall not be forgiven unto men. And whosoever speaketh a word against the Son of man, it shall be forgiven him: but whosoever speaketh against the Holy Ghost, it shall not be forgiven him, neither in this world, neither in the world to come.[43]

In Henry's Commentary (Henry [1708] 1960, p. 64), Henry explains that:

> blasphemy against the Holy Spirit is the only unpardonable sin. What is sin? It is speaking against the Holy Spirit. See what malignity there is in tongue sins, when the only art of the sin is so. But Jesus knew their thoughts.[44]

What Henry is highlighting here is that it was not the thinking ill of the Holy Spirit that is blasphemous, but the speaking of it, as otherwise very few people would be free of this guilt. Henry then states that:

---

41. Eddy 1910, pp. 46, 47.
42. Eddy 1910, p. 562.
43. KJV, Matt. xii. 31, 32.
44. Henry [1708] 1960, vol. I, p. 64.

> This blasphemy is excepted, not for any defect in the mercy of God or the merit in Christ, but because it inevitably leads the sinner in infidelity and impenitency.[45]

What Henry means is that, as the Holy Spirit is the 'active force' with the potential to provide salvation, 'There is no cure for a sin so directly against the remedy' (ibid., p. 64). The quotes below indicate that it would appear to exist in perpetuity:

> Verily I say unto you, All sins shall be forgiven unto the sons of men, and blasphemies wherewith soever they shall blaspheme: But he that shall blaspheme against the Holy Ghost hath never forgiveness, but is in danger of eternal damnation.[46]

> Also I say unto you, Whosoever shall confess me before men, him shall the Son of man also confess before the angels of God: But he that denieth me before men shall be denied before the angels of God. And whosoever shall speak a word against the Son of man, it shall be forgiven him: but unto him that blasphemeth against the Holy Ghost it shall not be forgiven.[47]

The relevance of this point is that it provides another of the many reasons that mainstream Christianity has been so hostile to Christian Science ever since it first appeared. Even the academic discipline of Religious Studies, normally distinguished from theology by its neutral stance towards the truth claims made by a particular religion, does not always achieve this neutrality when Christian Science is under consideration. This has compounded the historical injustice previously described, adding what might be termed academic religious prejudice to the philosophical dismissal of Eddy's ideas.

The similarities between Christian Science and some Eastern religions echoed a growing interest in the late nineteenth century in these previously poorly studied areas in the West, and particularly in Great Britain and the USA. This was exemplified by the World Parliament of Religions in Chicago in 1893, at which there were

---

45. Ibid., p. 64.
46. KJV: Mark iii. 28-30.
47. KJV: Luke xii. 8-10.

presentations on Vedanta philosophy and Theosophy. Christian Science, Vedanta philosophy and Theosophy all attracted strong followings amongst the intellectuals of the late nineteenth century, but Christian Scientists themselves, however, sought to differentiate between the philosophy of Eastern religions and that of their own, which they held to be fundamentally different, though this was only really true from roughly the mid-1880s onwards.

The many vocal critics of Christian Science during Eddy's lifetime caused the publication of numerous defences of her position, including several by Eddy herself. This subsection offers a selection of quotes from three works in which she sought to justify her counterintuitive system of thought: *No and Yes*; *Rudimental Divine Science*; and *Unity of Good*.

Regarding the nonexistence of matter:

> There is no material science. God is infinite Mind, hence there is no other mind. ... Spirit is not in matter, but in Spirit only. Law is not in matter, but in Mind only.[48]

Also:

> The five material senses testify to the existence of matter. The spiritual senses afford us no such evidence, but deny the testimony of the material senses. Which testimony is correct?... If, as the Scriptures imply. God is All-in-All, then all must be Mind, since God is Mind. Therefore in divine Science [i.e. in Christian Science] there is no material mortal man, for man is spiritual and eternal, he being made in the image of Spirit, or God.[49]

Additionally:

> God is All-in-all. Hence He is in Himself only, in His own nature and character, and is perfect being, or consciousness. He is all the Life and Mind there is or can be. Within Himself is every embodiment of Life and Mind.[50]

---

48. Eddy 1891b, p. 4.
49. Ibid., pp. 4, 5.
50. Eddy 1888, p. 3.

Note the very important distinction: Eddy is claiming that within God is every embodiment, not God within other things. This vital difference is between pantheism, which Eddy's critics accused her of, and panentheism, which was her actual position. Panentheism, as well as asserting that the world is within God (as opposed to God being present in all worldly objects), crucially maintains the separate identity of the non-Divine[51].

On the question of the nonexistence of illness (a good example of Eddy's denial of a common-sense view of reality):

> Disease is more than *imagination*; it is a human error, a constituent part of what comprise the whole of mortal existence, namely, material sensation and mental delusion… The error of belief, named disease, never made sickness a stubborn reality… the Science of Mind-healing destroys the feasibility of disease; hence error of thought becomes fable instead of fact. … Sin and disease are not scientific, because they embody not the idea of divine Principle, and are not phenomena of the immutable laws of God; and they do not arise from the divine consciousness and true constituency of being. The unreality of sin, disease, and death, rests on the exclusive truth that being, to be eternal, must be harmonious.[52]

Additionally:

> Christian Science refutes the validity of the testimony of the senses, which take cognizance of their own phenomena – sickness, disease, and death. … The evidence that the earth is motionless and the sun revolves around our planet, is as sensible and real as the evidence for disease; but Science determines the evidence in both cases to be unreal. … Astronomy, optics, acoustics, and hydraulics are all at war with the testimony of the physical senses. This fact intimates that the laws of Science are mental, not material; and Christian Science demonstrates this.[53]

---

51. Nikkel 1995, p. 4.
52. Eddy 1887a, p. 4.
53. Ibid., p. 6.

So the key point is that the evidence of spiritual sense is without error, but is drowned out in ordinary life by the conventional senses, i.e. in people unschooled in Christian Science. On the topic of the nonexistence of evil:

> Christian Science… gives the lie to sin, in the spirit of Truth; but other theories make sin true. … A lie is negation – *alias* nothing, or the opposite of something. named evil, must be… unreal.[54]

Further:

> As God is Mind, if this Mind is familiar with evil, all cannot be good therein. Our infinite model would be taken away. What is in eternal Mind must be reflected in man, Mind's image. How then could man escape, or hope to escape, from a knowledge which is as everlasting in his creator?[55]

So evil is illusory – an error of belief – but more than this, note Eddy's analysis of a lie as the opposite of something and therefore nothing. It is this argument which she applies to many human constructs, such as pain, illness and death, but beyond even these radical claims, to the entire physical universe and all its assumed characteristics.

Eddy and the problem of 1943

Just as it is possible to damn an individual with faint praise, it is equally feasible for it to occur in the presence of an excess of praise. Few philosophers in the 2600-year Western history of the subject have had to deal with being equated with Deity, but this is precisely what happened to Eddy's reputation in 1943. In that year the Board of Directors of the Church of Christ, Scientist, concluded that Mary Baker Eddy was the woman prophesied in the twelfth chapter of the Book of Revelation within the Christian Bible. This was revealed to the public in the 5 June 1943 edition of the *Christian Science Sentinel*, and was a source of heated controversy amongst Christian Scientists,

---

54. Ibid., p. 32.
55. Eddy 1888, p. 14.

let alone the wider public. Mainstream Christians in particular felt that this was tantamount to blasphemy, and more conservative elements within the Christian Science Church worried that it would bring their movement into disrepute and even ridicule. The following text on a still more extreme version of Eddy's true identity is taken from an editorial by the Christian Science teacher, Judge Septimus J. Hanna, CSD:

> A second coming is as clearly prophesied as was the first coming. The Old Testament writers foretold it, Jesus plainly prophesied it, and the apostles reiterated these prophecies. ... Only, as yet, a comparatively small part of mankind are ready to accept the larger coming comprehended in a re-establishment of the religious regime which Jesus inaugurated. This small part of mankind are [sic] satisfied that the second coming has commenced and is now manifesting itself in the works which Jesus taught should be evidence of the fact that the Kingdom of Heaven was at hand... Christian Scientists believe in a personal second coming [and] see in the non-acceptance of [Mary Baker Eddy and Christian Science] an almost literal repetition of early history... Christian Scientists [see] in Genesis a prophecy of the Second Coming in female form. In Revelation they see the finality of prophecy. To their understanding the Woman of the Apocalypse stands in type for the female of God's creation spoken of in Genesis. ... We believe Mary Baker Eddy represents the Second Coming of Christ.[56]

It is difficult to imagine that this decision encouraged the academic study of Eddy's work as philosophy.

The initial popularity of Christian Science

One reason which has been suggested for Christian Science's initial popularity and success in acquiring new members was that, until the discovery and introduction of antibiotics, conventional medicine

---

56. Hanna, S., quoted in *The Destiny of The Mother Church* by Bliss Knapp, pp. 271-97.

achieved very poor outcomes with regard to infectious illness, and what treatments were available were either unpleasant, harmful or both[57]. The occasional genuine cure (from a conventional medical standpoint) achieved by Christian Science practitioners, whatever its actual cause, was greatly welcomed by the patient and their family and friends, whereas those who were treated, but unfortunately did not benefit were not harmed by the 'treatment', which consisted solely of an explanation regarding the nonexistence of illness, followed by prayer.

The magnitude of potential harm which they were avoiding by not seeking contemporary medical attention can be judged by the fact that some medicines of the nineteenth century were based on arsenic, mercury and even strychnine, in the last case one of the most toxic alkaloids known either then or now. Additionally creating the greatest suffering before death, strychnine overdoses, a frequent and facile (mostly) unintentional outcome in Victorian times, kill by inducing cramp-level contractures of the entire body, including the muscles required for respiration, thus asphyxiating the patient.

Advances in medicine since the 1940s have presumably had a negative effect upon how Christian Science is generally perceived, and some extremely high profile, tragic cases in the late twentieth century, involving what was seen as a failure to obtain lifesaving medical interventions for children, have also had an impact. The underlying philosophy, however, is unchanged.

Christian Science, from its very beginnings, attracted an intellectual following, perhaps, at least in part, as a result of the highly counterintuitive philosophy upon which it is based; only those comfortable with pure abstraction and the rejection of the 'evidence' of the physical senses tended to join as members. Some of its followers in the first century of its existence were prominent members of British, Russian and American society, such as Nancy Astor, Sergei Prokofiev and Mary Pickford[58], although this demographic is somewhat less true today than it once was. A highly unusual but absolute rule affecting members of the Christian Science Church is that they must not publish or reveal in any other form the level of membership; it is therefore hard to assess the current level in 2025, but approximately 20 years ago it was believed to be below 100,000[59]. Although representing a

---

57. Gill 1998, p. 172.
58. Siewers 2019, p. 3.
59. Stark 1998, p. 191.

large percentage fall relative to the peak membership of 268,915 in 1936, it corresponds to the surprisingly small annual figure of roughly just over one per cent per year (assuming a current membership of 100,000), which is broadly commensurate with the fall in attendance at established Christian Churches.

What had led Eddy to these highly unusual views? How had her life experiences influenced a woman with no higher education to a wholehearted commitment to such an extreme abstraction? Later in the text, I will demonstrate how a consistent application of a very 'pure' idealism was absolutely central to the development of her ideas, and ultimately her entire system. Every aspect of Christian Science is in some way influenced by this idealism, and so this forms a natural framework for the exploration of her work.

Prior philosophical research

Although much has been written about Christian Science over the last 150 years, very little pertains to its underlying philosophy. Instead, histories of the Church and biographies of Mary Baker Eddy predominate, which although of interest are mostly somewhat tangential to the current topic; mostly, but not entirely.

Although Christian Scientists value the Bible and *Science and Health* equally, the theological terms Eddy used in *Science and Health* even when discussing Scripture do not necessarily have the same meaning as in mainstream, academic theology. It is vital, therefore, to understand precisely what is meant by apparently familiar terms when used in this technical manner, specific only to Christian Science. Failing to do so can lead theologians and other academics into publicly disagreeing, sometimes very forcefully and in print, with assertions which were not actually being made.

An excellent example of Eddy's curious choice of terms is her use of the word 'chemicalization', which she used to mean the process of realisation that what we believe to be matter is in actuality spirit. The word 'chemicalization' is therefore used to mean the opposite of what one might assume in three different ways simultaneously:

1. The word gives the impression that a process is taking place which will result in the production of chemicals of some unspecified form, or as a result of their presence, yet Christian Science occupies different magisteria;

2. The word conveys the idea of the existence of an objective, physical process, whereas Eddy's is referring to a subjective, mental one; and
3. In combination with the second word from the phrase 'Christian Science', the word 'chemicalization' immediately suggests that whatever it is that is being referred to is within the bounds of the academic discipline of chemistry, which in reality has no overlap with Eddy's system of thought.

Henry Steiger is one of the very few people who have addressed the philosophy of Christian Science. His 1946 Boston University PhD thesis, 'A Philosophical Investigation of the Doctrine of Christian Science', subsequently reworked as his 1948 book on the same subject[60], is a useful starting point, but is a little idiosyncratic in its coverage, perhaps as a result of Steiger's closeness to the Church of Christ, Scientist, of which he was a member.

Stephen Gottschalk's two principal works, *The Emergence of Christian Science in American Religious Life*, and more particularly *Rolling Away the Stone: Mary Baker Eddy's Challenge to Materialism*, provide partial analyses of the philosophy underpinning Christian Science. Broader and more detailed than Steiger's, they offer a less optimistic assessment; as mentioned earlier, Gottschalk[61] concluded that a 'closed metaphysical system' was 'impossible' to obtain from Eddy's writing, rather than attempting to create solutions to the difficulties which emerge as a result of such work.

A further barrier to the academic analysis of Christian Science is the nonlinear and disorderly aspects of Eddy's work, present to varying degrees throughout her many books. This does not diminish the originality or ingenuity of the concepts she describes, however; what it does require of the reader is the careful, piece-by-piece assembly of a coherent, macro-level expression of her system from the micro-level arguments which are present. This task, together with equally careful comparisons and contrasts with the ideas of others who were approximately contemporaneous with Eddy, will form the majority of the next chapter.

---

60. Steiger 1948.
61. 1973, p. 33.

Chapter 3

Eddy Viewed from Near and Far

Satter

Beryl Satter and Amy Voorhees have recently contributed highly significant additions to the body of literature on Eddy's work. Satter's recent work, *Each Mind a Kingdom* provides a treasure trove of detailed information specific to Evans and Quimby and their ideas. Both Evans and Quimby had provided elements of the foundational concepts upon which Eddy went on to build her system of thought, and Evans and Eddy initially shared a set of questions, such as what is the relationship between God and mind? Is mind in matter or separate from it? Should mind be thought of as masculine or feminine? Should matter be thought of as masculine or feminine?

Evans concluded that man is equivalent to spirit and woman to matter, and beyond this that the 'mental' is scientific and desire the 'divine spark'. Eddy, of course, denied the existence of matter entirely[1]. Quimby, with whom both Eddy and Evans had studied, believed that the 'false opinions' of priests implanted fears, and that this continual 'background' worry led to illness. For example, the Calvinist concept that some people are predestined to go to hell at the end of their earthly existence, irrespective of their conduct on earth and utterly beyond their control, would understandably be of very great concern to those with an absolute belief in its complete truth;

---

1. Satter 1999, p. 70.

it must be remembered that hell in this case is understood to involve infinite agony for all eternity.

During the 1850s and 1860s, Evans offered new interpretations of familiar Bible stories, demonstrably improving the lives of those who heard them. He gave public demonstrations that, at least in some cases, the experience of illness could be eliminated by 'reasoning them [his patients] away from such false beliefs'[2]. Unlike Eddy, Evans did not deny the existence of matter, instead considering it as an emanation from God and existing in a set of hierarchical states – mineral, vegetable and animal – with developmental progress being governed by 'spiritual force', which he equated with revelation from God. He believed that humanity must seek to escape matter and become 'transparent to spirit'[3], with 'science' meaning 'spiritual knowledge' and therefore with God as the 'master scientist'. Matter, for Evans, was affected by emotion, and the emotions, he claimed, could be shaped by thought, although, in a puzzlingly contradictory analysis, he also claimed that, as an emanation of God, matter must already be perfect. Humanity's task, he claimed, is to acquire divine powers, with this being the true meaning of salvation. This was where Eddy most vehemently disagreed with Evans, as his suggestion that mankind might develop Godlike power was for her the worst heresy, even blasphemy, Eddy instead envisaging a world in which no one would be 'subject to birth, growth, maturity and decay', but instead reside within a 'painless and permanent' sphere[4].

Voorhees

Amy Voorhees is an independent scholar who in both her PhD thesis and the subsequent book based upon it (Voorhees 2021) traces the development of Christian Science, contextualising it within the theological movements of the late nineteenth century and detailing the evolution of Eddy's unique understanding of Christianity. Voorhees has – in addition to superbly augmenting the scholarship regarding Eddy's history, her ideas and the context within which she developed them – drawn attention to the great contemporary interest in the two varieties of the theological concept of millennialism in

---

2. Ibid., p. 60.
3. Ibid., p. 61.
4. Ibid., p. 77.

the New England of Eddy's time. Pre-millennialism refers to the idea of Christ returning before the Kingdom of God appears on earth, whereas post-millennialism describes the situation where Christ returns once the Kingdom of God has arrived. Crucially, in both cases, these were thought of as future events, but as Voorhees points out, Eddy does not 'fit neatly' into either 'dichotomous option' (Voorhees 2021, p. 100) of millennialism then offered as explanatory frameworks regarding Christ's return. Instead, Eddy thought of the Kingdom of God 'appearing in human consciousness to transform earthly experience *now*' (Voorhees 2021, p. 100, my italics), perfection already being present, but the human realisation of it only gradual. This is a further demonstration of Eddy's originality and prescience; it is only very recently that modern scholarship has returned to serious consideration of the theological position known as preterism, which is the closest that mainstream theology comes to coinciding with this element of Eddy's thought.

Voorhees is also very helpful in summarising Jonathan Edwards' role in shaping Eddy's ideas. Edwards' *A History of the Work of Redemption* presents arguments based on texts from the books of Daniel and Revelation to establish the beginning of the millennium (the 1000-year period involved in all Christian eschatology) as beginning either in the mid-nineteenth century or very early in the twenty-first, with 1866 being specifically mentioned. Bearing in mind the year of Eddy's fall on ice was 1866, it is unsurprising that she was influenced by this and the calculation of other dates, such as those shown diagrammatically by Frank Messenger in *Time of the End* (1856) and referred to by Voorhees[5].

Braude

Ann Braude has also contributed to the recently renewed interest in scholarship concerning Eddy, which has particularly accelerated in the first two decades of the twenty-first century[6]. However, her work is less relevant to a philosophical text than that of Satter and Voorhees, and so will not be considered here beyond acknowledging its existence and the contextualisation it provides for Eddy's oeuvre.

---

5. Voorhees 2021, p. 102.
6. Braude 2007.

Twain

Mark Twain, like Eddy, had deduced to his own satisfaction that an omnipotent and omniscient God of love could not coexist with human pain and suffering. This is analogous with C.S. Lewis' argument for the divinity of Christ (known as the Lewis Trilemma, in which we are forced to accept His divinity or dismiss Him as either insane or satanic; there is no middle ground remaining)[7]. For Lewis, in the case of Christ, the option of regarding him as merely a great moral teacher 'is not left open to us'[8] whereas with Eddy's system and the idea of pain, one either chooses God and the unreality of pain, or suffering and the absence of God. For Eddy, of course, it was the former, but for Twain, who had in 1909 recently lost both his wife and daughter, the overwhelming reality of grief was evidence of God's nonexistence. Intriguingly, Twain's bitterness towards these events in his life ultimately led him to a far more extreme denial of physicalist ontology than his initial metaphysics-denying response of atheism, albeit in a work of fiction. In his last novel, *No. 44, The Mysterious Stranger*, the last chapter reveals an extraordinary truth, almost fully in keeping with that of Gorgias the Nihilist: 'Life itself is only a vision, a dream… Nothing exists save empty space – and you!'[9].

Representative critical literature and difficulties inherent in the analysis of Eddy's work

One form of literature regarding Christian Science of which there is absolutely no shortage is that which is critical of Mary Baker Eddy either personally or in relation to the system of belief constituted by Christian Science. Much of it was written in the late nineteenth century or the first decade of the twentieth century when Mary Baker Eddy was still alive. Incredulous and sometimes even hysterical in tone, these works gave Eddy herself the opportunity to tackle the individual areas of misunderstanding which they represent by writing a series of monographs on specific topics. These, and others by a range of authors, were made available by the Christian Science

---

7. Lewis 1952, pp. 54-56.
8. Lewis 1952, p. 56.
9. Twain 1916, p. 65.

Church's own publishing company and continued to be produced on single subjects in the years following Eddy's death.

As well as introducing original ideas of her own, Eddy's works utilise forms of idealism which were already well known at the time she was writing. Although initially acknowledging the similarities between her principal work, *Science and Health*, and the Hindu philosophy expressed in the Upanishads (and other Hindu and Buddhist works), she removed this acknowledgement from later editions of the same text. There is also some similarity between *Science and Health* and the work of the American transcendentalists, such as Emerson, Thoreau and Alcott[10], though it is clear that only the books of the last of these was known to Eddy, and even in this case only to the very slightest degree. Other forms of idealism, however, are also present within her various works, with concepts from the absolute idealism of Hegel, the subjective idealism of Fichte and the idiosyncratic idealisms of von Hardenberg and Schleiermacher, amongst several others. This is an important aspect with regard to elevating Eddy's standing as a philosopher, so although these other forms of idealism will not be described here, it is the fact of their existence which needs to be acknowledged at this early stage in the analysis. The problem in identifying these and other forms of idealism in Eddy's writing is that, in addition to the previously mentioned nebulousness and variable logical structure, she defined a lexicon specific to Christian Science in which many familiar words from theology, philosophy and psychology are used to convey sometimes very different meanings to those which are conventionally the case. A considerable familiarity with Christian Science is therefore a prerequisite to any further philosophical analysis and may further explain the dearth of academic works on this sadly neglected subject, due to the completely understandable misinterpretation by highly skilled, academic philosophers regarding its true originality and subtlety.

In this overview of the relevant literature specific to Christian Science, I have begun to demonstrate that although there is a wealth of material regarding Mary Baker Eddy's life and work, there is an extraordinary lack of serious philosophical analysis. As a consequence, I will of necessity include a considerable quantity of non-specific texts which will assist in the analysis of Eddy's work.

---

10. Grodzins 2002, p. 64.

Many texts concerning Eddy's life and work can be of value, including some whose true value is quite counterintuitive. This section demonstrates the sheer variety and novelty of sources which may assist this research.

Parker

Theodore Parker was a highly influential ordained scholar who campaigned for women's rights and the abolition of slavery, and who also gave sermons in which he expressed doubts regarding Biblical authority and the historicity of Scriptural miracles. He is often quoted today without the realisation of his authorship, for example in his definition of democracy as 'government of all the people, by all the people, for all the people'. His ideas provide a useful context within which to frame Eddy's concepts and beyond which to note their originality. Parker, in common with other Unitarians, believed that 'supernatural rationalism' was needed in order to determine religious truths, meaning that the 'natural religion' of reason is incomplete without the 'revealed religion' of the Bible, for example regarding Christ's role and his miracles. Parker held that an analogy could be drawn between the laws of matter and the 'laws of spirit' on the basis that both were created by God, both are changeless and both are eternal. He believed that the greater the closeness with which one adheres to these spiritual laws, the greater the level of potential inspiration, offering the possibility that contemporary or future writers might demonstrate equal or even greater inspiration than was evidenced by the historic writers of Scripture. In the latter half of the 1830s, Parker's ideas began to coincide with those of the American transcendentalists, resulting in him attending meetings of the Transcendental Club and, by the 1840s, publishing many articles in *The Dial*, the principal journal of American transcendentalist thought[11].

Twain again

Twain harboured an extraordinary level of cognitive dissonance regarding Eddy, the following two quotes illustrating the extreme dichotomy of what he appeared to believe concurrently. Regarding

---

11. Grodzins 2002, pp. 110 ff.

Christian Science, 'it has the same value now as when Mrs. Eddy stole it from Quimby... Mrs. Eddy the fraud, the humbug...'[12] and: 'Christian Science is humanity's boon. Mother Eddy deserves a place in the Trinity as much as any of any member of it. She has organized and made available a healing principle that for two thousand years has never been employed, except as the merest kind of guesswork. She is the benefactor of our age'[13]. This sort of polarisation of two opposed opinions is commonplace within a population, but rare within a single individual, and especially when simultaneous.

Georgine Milmine

Milmine's work[14] is helpful in that it focusses on the differences between Mary Baker Eddy's understanding of Christian Science and that of some of her dissenting or defecting former students. One example is that of Josephine Woodbury, who was a Christian Science student of Eddy between 1884 and 1885, but in 1886 opened her own 'Massachusetts Academy of Christian Science'. Woodbury's intention, unlike many other defectors, was not to create a rival organisation but to promote Christian Science, albeit in her own, heavily augmented form. It is the detail between these different systems which Milmine covers so well, although it is worth noting that Gottschalk states that the work is 'copiously documented, but heavily biased against its subject'[15].

Edwin Franklin Dakin

The title of Dakin's biography of Eddy, *Eddy: The Biography of a Virginal Mind*[16] provides potential readers with a prior warning as to its sensationalist tone and debunking nature, largely the same in character, although not with regard to either level of detail or overall length, as Milmine's biography. Dakin generously praises Milmine's work as being 'so detailed and annotated that it is nothing short of

---

12. quoted in Paine 1912 vol. 2, p. 247.
13. quoted in Bigelow 1912 vol. 3, p. 1271.
14. Milmine 1909.
15. Gottschalk 1973, p. 160.
16. Dakin 1929, 1930.

a monumental piece of work'[17] and Milmine herself as 'an intrepid, path-breaking researcher'[18].

Albert Einstein

In as much as Einstein ever discussed theological and philosophical matters, his outlook was broadly Quakerly with regard to theology and Spinozian regarding philosophy[19]. However, an until recently little-researched area of his interests late in life was Christian Science, or, more accurately, the philosophy underlying its relation to Einstein's physics. Parallels with the illusory nature of matter and the absence of an observer-independent frame of reference led him to remark in 1952, '... to think a woman knew this 80 years ago'[20]. Einstein visited his local Christian Science Reading Room a number of times and stated that 'If I were not a Jew I would be a Christian Scientist'[21].

Emma Curtiss Hopkins

Emma Curtiss Hopkins met Eddy in 1883, taking a class at her suggestion between December 1883 and January 1884, at which time she wrote that 'I lay my life all talents, little or great, to this work.' Appointed by Eddy in September 1884 as the editor of the *Journal of Christian Science* (later renamed the *Christian Science Journal*), she remained in post between 1884 and 1885, and was therefore well-placed to comment on both Christian Science and Mary Baker Eddy more personally. Hopkins stated that Eddy 'clearly considered herself to be a revelatory prophet on a divine mission, functioning on a path parallel to the prevailing patriarchal system'[22]. It is this critical and analytical closeness which enabled Hopkins to make useful observations on the philosophy of Christian Science, particularly given the fact of her later firing by Eddy from her position as editor following Hopkins' claiming that she was in direct communion with

---

17. Dakin 1930, p. 418.
18. Ibid., p. 418.
19. Isaacson 2008, pp. 388-89.
20. Keyston 1996, p. 189.
21. Clark 2007, p. 622.
22. Hopkins 1888 p. 177.

God regarding the new metaphysics. Subsequently to her dismissal by Eddy, Hopkins moved to Chicago (unusually for the era, without her husband and son) and began teaching her own version of a metaphysical healing system, forming the Hopkins Metaphysical Association for this purpose. This endeavour initially expanded faster than Eddy's Christian Science Church, in that within three years Hopkins had at least seventeen branches of her association operating throughout the USA and had personally taught over 600 students[23].

Given the nature of her separation from Christian Science, it is unsurprising that Hopkins' metaphysics differed markedly from Eddy's. Profound examples include the fact that Hopkins viewed divine Mind as masculine, with what she termed 'carnal mind' as feminine and 'akin to a window or a mirror'[24], and her understanding of the belief in evil being 'part of God's plan' and a 'mentally created evil'[25] implanted by mainstream Christianity. A further departure from Eddy was on a social issue. Hopkins' feminism concerned equality, and she was 'energetically devoted to feminism among other social reforms'[26], whereas Eddy's interest was in what women were (and would) achieve alone.

Karl Barth

Although the theologian Karl Barth considered that Christian Science theology has certain features in common with the New Testament, he also held that there was an important point of absolute difference: 'God is indeed the basis of all reality... but He is not the only reality. As a Creator and Redeemer He loves a reality which is different from himself, which depends upon him, but which is not merely a reflection nor the sum of his powers and thoughts'[27]. It is by detailing these differences that Barth is so helpful, the above quote being just an example.

---

23. Satter 1999, p. 81.
24. Ibid., p. 87.
25. Ibid., p. 86.
26. Gottschalk 2006, p. 181.
27. Barth 1936, vol. I, p. 159.

Georgie Sheldon

Georgie Sheldon (no known relation of the author) had worked as a novelist for some decades when she embarked on writing *Katherine's Sheaves*[28] which although a work of fiction is nevertheless of relevance to and is used by the present text because of the subject matter and its precise handling. The novel centres on a new student at an all-female college, who, owing to the combination of her adoption of Christian Science and the religiously conservative ethos of the college, encounters frequent resistance to her academic progress. The setting of the novel affords Sheldon the opportunity to involve the central character in lengthy, highly thoughtful and well-argued discussions with other students and, particularly, other staff; the novel can be seen as simply being a vehicle for these expositions of Christian Science beliefs and practices.

Summary

Atypical sources of information on a subject are not necessarily of less value than those which come from more commonly expected sources. In some cases, the material provided by these sometimes surprising texts can be of greater value than conventional ones, being better expressed, more informed and, in rare cases, both. In the case of Mary Baker Eddy this is particularly true, as biographical texts have a hagiographic tendency, and standard works on the beliefs and history of the Christian Science Church have broadly the same structure and content as each other and lack much detail regarding the underlying philosophy. The best example of the usefulness of atypical sources is *Katherine's Sheaves* (Sheldon 1904), which is almost the opposite case to that of standard works: expositions of the justifications for Christian Science beliefs are present in quantity and quality.

---

28. Sheldon 1904.

Chapter 4

Robert Peel and the Conceptual Bridge

The work of Robert Peel provides the conceptual bridge between Eddy's philosophical system and its application as a form of healing. A lifelong Christian Scientist himself, Peel could see both sides of this divide in his daily life. His three-volume biography of Eddy is by far the longest and most detailed of any written so far, and the many healings of which he had direct experience led him to pursue analytically the challenge Christian Science clearly presents to a conventional understanding of the physical sciences, such as physics, chemistry and biology. Peel's life spanned all ten decades of the twentieth century, beginning in 1909 in the London of Edwardian England, and ending in Boston, Massachusetts in 1992.

Peel's biography of Eddy is impressive in both its breadth and depth, and it is obvious where the material is factual as opposed to where it is his expressed opinion. For this reason, critics who have focussed on what they saw as an apologist element of his writing could be seen as unfairly dismissing the work. The degree of scholarship is profound, resulting in insights which are not present in other similar works, and references are made throughout to source material which was newly available at the time of his writing. His extraordinarily generous interpretation of certain events in Eddy's life is easily delineated from the rest and does not diminish it.

Although Peel is best known for his three-volume biography, *Mary Baker Eddy: The Years of Discovery* (1966), *Mary Baker Eddy: The Years of Trial* (1971), and *Mary Baker Eddy: The Years of Authority* (1977), his other works are of equal value outside the biographical sphere, *Spiritual Healing in a Scientific Age* (Peel 1987) being of particular relevance to this work.

The greatest value of Peel's contribution to the growing scholarship regarding Christian Science lies in its linking of the fundamental principles discovered by Mary Baker Eddy and their application to the specific form of healing with which the Church is associated. Peel's immense knowledge of the subject and of Eddy herself, combined with his lifelong experience as a Christian Scientist, serves to unify the highly abstract nature of the idealist philosophy underpinning Christian Science with its unique understanding of and approach to illness.

Peel expressed his beliefs in careful detail, an example being below:

> In the ministry of healing, as in the worship of God, it is evident that the Father's house has many rooms.
>
> Within the Christian tradition the pastoral counselor, the charismatic faith healer, the Christian Science practitioner, and the priest anointing the sick with oil have at least three things in common. They have the inspiration of a common Lord and Master, a common conviction that the ministry of healing and the worship of God are profoundly related, and a common purpose to bring to the sufferer not merely bodily well-being but genuine spiritual health.
>
> In considering the distinctive role of the Christian Science practitioner, a few preliminary facts may be useful.
>
> Christian Science, although best known for its healing work, is also a way of life, a religious discipline, a metaphysical study, a denominational structure. In one sense, every Christian Scientist is expected to be a practitioner of his religion – that is, to prove his faith and understanding by his works. Like the moral and spiritual regeneration to which it is closely allied, healing is regarded as the natural fruit of drawing closer to God.
>
> Yet it is obvious that those who encounter apparently insuperable obstacles in their endeavor to do this need expert help. In such cases they may turn to an experienced Christian Scientist who, on a professional basis, devotes his full time to the ministry of healing in its broadest sense. This is the Christian Science practitioner properly so called,

and his is a religious vocation to which any committed and qualified Christian Scientist can aspire.[1]

Robert Peel was born in London in 1909 to Anne Susannah Monk, a Christian Scientist, and Arthur James Peel, before later moving to Boston with his parents and sister in the early 1920s. In 1927 he began studying English literature at Harvard University, graduating in 1931, with his undergraduate honours thesis, *The Creed of a Victorian Pagan*, a study of English poet and novelist George Meredith, being the only undergraduate thesis published by the university that year.

After graduating, Peel taught history and literature at Harvard and began his graduate studies, although his 1935 proposal for a doctorate on Mary Baker Eddy was rejected by the university. After several years teaching at Harvard, Peel taught philosophy and English at Principia College, a Christian Science college in Illinois, returning to Harvard in 1940 for his master's degree, followed by the resumption of his teaching at Principia.

After the war, Peel joined *The Christian Science Monitor*, a newspaper founded and wholly owned by the Christian Science Church, writing book reviews and editorials, before leaving in 1953 to begin working for The First Church of Christ, Scientist itself, at the Church's central administration in Boston, Massachusetts, where he was appointed as an advisor to the Church's Committee on Publication. That year, he wrote and recorded a radio talk about Christian Science, 'Moving Mountains', which was first published in *The Christian Science Monitor*, and subsequently in the prestigious BBC magazine *The Listener*. In the article, he presented the case for the Christian Science understanding of humanity as 'spiritual rather than material, incapable of corruption and error, no more subject to annihilation than his Maker'.

His first book, *Christian Science: Its Encounter with American Culture*, was published in 1958, but his extensive research into the life of Mary Baker Eddy, continued and deepened, culminating in his biographical trilogy, *Mary Baker Eddy: The Years of Discovery* (1966), *Mary Baker Eddy: The Years of Trial* (1971), and *Mary Baker Eddy: The Years of Authority* (1977), first published by Holt, Rinehart

---

1. Peel 1969, pp. 39-42.

and Winston and subsequently by the Christian Science Publishing Society.

Cornelius J. Dyck, a theologian, considered Peel's approach in *Christian Science: Its Encounter with American Culture* (1958) as being 'partisan but gentle, the intention is apologetic but without either alienating the reader or making a wild-eyed convert out of him'. Peel's exceptionally detailed research subsequently led to a possible reduction from total objectivity, as witnessed by Charles S. Braden in his review of *Mary Baker Eddy: The Years of Discovery*, writing in 1967:

> Despite the impressive apparatus of scholarship employed, Mr. Peel's book must be taken for what it really is, an exceedingly clever piece of propaganda in support of the official view of the life of Mrs. Eddy. As such it is probably the most effective that has yet appeared.[2]

In a similar vein, the historian James Findlay wrote that Peel was 'highly sympathetic' to Eddy; and that what emerged was a 'flat, one or two-dimensional image that remains unreal'. However, in spite of this, Findlay concluded that *The Years of Discovery* as a 'substantial addition to the literature on American religious history'.

Raymond J. Cunningham, a history professor at Fordham University, described Peel the following year as a 'painstaking and imaginative scholar' and the final book of Peel's trilogy as a more balanced picture of Eddy, but noted his 'uncomfortably reverential' approach and special pleading to resolve 'doubtful points in favor of the subject'. Despite this, Cunningham stated that the work represented an important achievement, although the biographer Carol Dickson claimed that 'Peel seeks to ignore controversies completely by confining discussions of conflicting evidence and questions of reliability to his notes.'

Many differing opinions on Peels work existed contemporaneously with those above. Martin E. Marty[3] wrote in the *New York Times Book Review* that Peel's work had 'begun to break the barriers between apologists and critics'. Gillian Gill glowingly described Peel as 'Mrs. Eddy's most brilliant, informed, and judicious biographer'[4] and

---

2. Braden 1967.
3. Marty 1978, p. 41.
4. Gill 1998, p. 40.

additionally said that 'Throughout the biography his love, sympathy, and reverence for his subject shine through', and furthermore that 'Peel was also dedicated to historical truth and serious scholarship, and his text is supplemented by references, quotations, and copious notes which form a treasure trove for scholars'[5].

If there is one thing which equalled Eddy's intellectual energy, it is her zeal for her discovery to be of use. Her dismissal of existing academic philosophy was largely on the basis of what she saw as its inapplicability in everyday life, something which cannot be said of her intentions for either *Science and Health* or the Massachusetts Metaphysical College. Apart from surgery, medicine of the late nineteenth and early twentieth century was largely ineffective, antibiotics only becoming available to physicians during World War 2 and not being generally available until after its end. Worse still, many pharmaceuticals of the era did not conform to the Hippocratic principle of 'First, do no harm', instead involving toxic quantities of a great variety of compounds, even including radioactive elements, such as radium. Just how disastrous this last example is can be judged by the fact that, as a member of Group 2 of the periodic table, which includes calcium, it is therefore a 'bone-seeker', becoming integrated into the calcium-based matrix of bones throughout the body, where it unleashes its radiation; the consequences are of course bone cancers.

Surgery at this time was also risky. In the absence of antibacterials, post-operative infections could be rapidly fatal, and before about 1950, the administration of muscle relaxants was not part of anaesthetic practice, necessitating a much deeper level of anaesthesia and thereby a greater risk of complications or death. Just how many patients Mary Baker Eddy saved from the conventional medicine of her period is hard to estimate, but the reduction in suffering is easy to imagine. Peel's thoughts on Eddy are superbly summarised in the following quote:

> A 1948 academic study (Steiger) concluded that Eddy had done something new by evolving a metaphysic that healed. She herself claimed that physical healing was the 'least part' of Christian Science, subordinate to the whole process of spiritual regeneration. But she also saw it as an essential element of the kerygma 'scientifically' understood. As Science

---

5. Gill 1998, p. 581.

and Health puts it: 'The Word was made flesh.' Divine Truth must be known by its effects on the body as well as on the mind, before the Science of Being can be demonstrated. Hence its embodiment in the incarnate Jesus, – that life-link forming the connection through which the real reaches the unreal, Soul rebukes sense, and Truth destroys error.

Eddy was of course not the first to think of Christianity as science and of God as principle. Not only the early church fathers, but also such later giants as Aquinas and Calvin used these terms. But that was before the immense sophistication of modern scientific method, rooted in controlled experiment and empirical verification, changed their meaning. Eddy realized that without the pragmatic component no religious system could claim to be scientific. Hence her emphasis on spiritual healing as the crucial evidence of the substantiality of Spirit in a world increasingly looking for causality in matter....

Though many people turn to Christian Science in the first place for healing of mind, body, or human situation, those who accept it as a permanent way of life are apt to regard such healing as a confirmatory sign rather than an end in itself. This at least is the ideal. From its earliest days there have been adherents who have wanted to turn it into a faith healing cult, a smart success philosophy, or a revival of second-century Gnosticism. So far none have succeeded. Eventually they all run up against the tenacious Christianity of the movement's founder who, through her writings, still shapes Christian Science thinking. Her concern extended far beyond the healing of physical ailments, as illustrated by her founding of The Christian Science Monitor in 1908 to help bring Christian values to bear in a healing way on the larger ills of the world.[6]

This quote is of great importance. Although Mary Baker Eddy was a pragmatist and practical individual, she was also a deep and profoundly original thinker; the mental and spiritual, for Eddy, as a philosophical idealist, *were* the world. Herein lies a possible resolution as to how the 'healing truth which dawned' upon her in the ice and snow of a nineteenth-century New England winter, could be both the

---

6. Peel 1969, pp. 39-42.

'least part' of Christian Science and yet *all of it*; the *entire universe* of creation reimagined.

Hegel believed himself to be the culmination of all human history; Eddy believed that her discovery (her preferred word) of Christian Science would be of the greatest value of all to humankind. 'Going beyond the data' may be true of both individuals, but it is this unblinkered zeal for the truly new which permits those few who create or discover it to have the confidence, perseverance and discipline needed to pursue their projects to fruition. Interestingly, all three of these qualities are described abundantly in Peel's biography, additionally being present in all three volumes.

An important aspect of Eddy's life's work has not yet been addressed here: why, after her spiritual discoveries were published for the world in *Science and Health with Key to the Scriptures*, did she put such effort into founding a Church?

In recent decades, spiritual authority in general has been under vitriolic attack by a newly militant band of atheist public intellectuals, and the Church of Christ, Scientist, is particularly a target in America. When she first wrote *Science and Health*, Eddy did not think that a new Church would be needed in order to redirect human thought to a correct understanding and demonstration of her radical spiritual philosophy. Yet just four years later she determined it to be essential, as part of God's plan for her discovery, to form the Church of Christ, Scientist – a Church 'designed to commemorate the word and works of our Master, which should reinstate primitive Christianity and its lost element of healing."

Many people were attracted to her teachings but ended up as believers in a myriad of distorted, individualised versions of Christian Science that were neither Christian nor scientific. The Church, therefore, was vital in both the promotion of true Christian Science and the ongoing defence against the corruption of its ideas.

John V. Dittemore, a prominent Christian Scientist, at the end of his life wrote that:

> God's law does not divide and separate men, it unites them, enabling them to work together and perpetuates this unity. ... It annihilates everything unlike itself and I find it has destroyed all sense of personal animosity, all desire to justify self.[7]

---

7. Dittemore in Beasley 1957, pp. 376-77.

The Church, for Eddy, was not an institutional structure but the human expression of God's care. Her intention for it is evident in her statement:

> Of this I am sure, that each Rule and By-law in this Manual will increase the spirituality of him who obeys it, invigorate his capacity to heal the sick, to comfort such as mourn, and to awaken the sinner.[8]

Peel's book, *Spiritual Healing in a Scientific Age*, is unique in bringing two subjects together. In it, he explores the connection between modern scientific assumptions and the ever-growing evidence for spiritual healing. As Peel observed,

> The word 'spiritual' is meaningless to many natural scientists today. ... To regard spirit or mind – let alone the Holy Spirit or Divine Mind – as an entity or power operating through higher laws to overrule and alter the perceived mechanism of the physical universe is therefore to invite instant dismissal by a large part of the scientific community. 'Where is your evidence?' they quite naturally ask, and often with considerable scorn. That is the question to which the rest of this book addresses itself.[9]

Both theologians and scientists are involved with questions regarding the nature of reality and meaning, but even in a time of increasing interdisciplinary study, there remains a separation of spiritual or religious questions from those which are empirical. Peel's focus on the healing effects of spiritual experience therefore rejects this separation. He considers the evidence for spiritual healing seriously, and also explores how this evidence questions certain scientific and medical assumptions.

Alcott wrote that:

> Any touch of idealism, however dashed with superstition, [and] over-clouded with mysticism, is to be regarded as a wholesome omen in these times of shallow materialism [Alcott is using the philosophical meaning of the word,

---

8. Eddy 1913, p. 230.
9. Peel 1987, p. 8.

rather than its modern association with wealth and that which wealth can buy] and atheistic dogmatism, in which so many indulge.[10]

Peel commented on this topic, stating that:

> In the eyes of Christian Scientists his idealism is tainted with what might be called the ultimate refinement of materialism, a sort of homeopathic attenuation of it to the point where matter very nearly disappears as a component of absolute reality, but remains as a necessary limitation on the power of Spirit.[11]

And further, that:

> Here, Alcott himself shows that 'common sense' which Emerson considered the mark of all valid minds and which he defined as the perception of matter.[12]

Common sense, however, can be very wrong indeed. One only has to consider the fact that even conventional physics asserts that less than one part in a trillion of what we think of as solid matter is other than empty space, or the Einsteinian understanding that the *distance* between two points can be different depending on the velocity of an observer.

Over half of Peel's *Spiritual Healing in a Scientific Age* consists of concrete examples of physical healing, supported by affidavits provided by direct participants in the healing experiences described. A great variety of medically diagnosed illnesses and disorders are covered, with virtually all subsequently involving spiritual healing as practised by Christian Scientists.

These testimonies of Christian Science healing relate to some of the most fundamental questions regarding the nature of reality itself. As Peel noted:

> Twentieth-century physics suggests that reality may be different from that posited by the reductionist, determinist, or

---

10. Alcott, quoted in Peel 1958, p. 87.
11. Peel 1958, p. 88.
12. Ibid., p. 88.

'scientific' materialism of the past – and posited still by the biomedical hardliner of today.[13]

Peel's purpose in writing the book was to introduce the type of data that the genuinely scientific spirit must acknowledge. The book presents the challenge to that spirit to take the evidence for spiritual healing seriously:

> The same adventurous spirit that has powered this century's scientific and technological triumphs can and must be brought to the fresh exploration of its neglected spiritual resources.[14]

Here we see the interplay of the two magisteria. The criteria of validity upon each of these arguably wholly separate stages is made evident so clearly as to be undeniable; those who seek to assert otherwise are not truly fair to either the other's data or their field of endeavour. The extraordinary quantity of successful healings, described in great detail both before and after the healing, cannot be ignored, even if one wing of the extremes of physical science would wish it to be so. This dichotomy has been of great concern to many thinkers since the time of Ancient Greece, and no doubt long before to the undocumented generations which preceded them.

How are we to reconcile such seemingly incompatible models of reality ourselves? This question hides two possible untruths: firstly, do we need to achieve this reconciliation? And secondly, is such a reconciliation necessary or even possible?

If Mary Baker Eddy is correct, then much or even all of what we are taught to believe as being true of the hypothetically asserted physical universe is false. Reconciling a wholly false understanding of the universe with one which is true would be impossible, and purposeless, even if it could be achieved.

Later in this book, the discussion moves on to how an erroneous analysis of Christian Science prompted by the COVID-19 pandemic could misrepresent its underlying principles almost in their entirety.

---

13. Peel 1987, p. 194.
14. Peel quoted in Gottschalk 1987, p. 42.

Chapter 5

The Philosophical Analysis of Christian Science

Forms of idealism applicable to the philosophical analysis of Eddy's work

In this section an exploration and analysis will be made of the great variety of texts on philosophical idealism which are helpful in achieving the goals of this book.

Introduction

A multiplicity of relevant general texts exist concerning idealism which are of obvious use in assisting with the identification of idealism in Mary Baker Eddy's writing. Narrowing the remit concerning these general texts on idealism is essential, as the field is far too large to conveniently survey and only certain types of idealism are helpful for this analysis. For this reason I will focus on similarities between Eddy's work and a carefully selected, small set of mostly German and British idealist philosophers.

Berkeley

Berkeley is the obvious starting point for a source of theoretical material regarding idealism (Berkeley 1710), but it is the differences between Eddy and Berkeley which are of issue.

Kant

Curiously, Kant can be a source of misunderstanding with reference to Eddy's idealism, as throughout her work, Eddy uses the word 'transcendental' in the manner adopted by the American transcendentalists, rather than in the more familiar Kantian meaning. Although Kant's use of the word 'transcendental' in 'transcendental idealism' refers to the distinction between the experienced world and the world beyond, he did not deny the reality of our experience, whereas Eddy's system does; and Kant claimed that we cannot have definite knowledge of the suprasensible world, whereas Eddy's 'spiritual sense', within her system, provides this directly[1].

Fichte

Gottlieb Fichte, beginning as a talented follower of Kant, soon developed his own original system, the *Wissenschaftslehre*[2], which adapted the precise meaning of the word 'transcendental'. Fichte argued that there are only two possible starting points for a system of philosophy, which he described as pure 'selfhood' and pure 'thinghood'. By this he meant idealism, in the former case, and what he termed 'dogmatism', in the latter, dogmatism being his negative epithet for any philosophical system involving the-thing-in-itself. In *Wissenschaftslehre* he explained that no 'mixed' system is possible, and that as no 'dogmatic' system can account for consciousness and all its corollaries, idealism is the only coherent solution. Very unusually, however, he conceived any constructed system as having the status of a hypothesis which must face subsequent testing; an intriguing parallel with Eddy clearly exists here regarding her understanding of 'healings' as providing evidence supporting her initial hypotheses.

Fichte conceived the 'I' as following from the act of its own positing (though actually simultaneously), with the *Anstoß* (the 'not-I') not external to the 'I' but created by it. He concluded that although philosophy could deduce the fact of spatial extension, the existence of time and the principle of causality, it had in certain areas very clearly

---

1. Martin 1955, p. 41.
2. Fichte 1797.

defined limits; the properties of individual objects, for example, are outside its remit.

Schopenhauer was deeply critical of Fichte's approach, stating that: 'He declared everything a priori, naturally without any evidence for such a monstrous assertion... [and] he appealed openly and boldly to intellectual intuition, that is, really to inspiration'[3]. Again, this is highly reminiscent of Eddy's understanding of Christian Science as revealed truth which she was inspired to write for the benefit of others.

Novalis

The early German idealists, Fichte and von Hardenberg (who wrote under the pseudonym Novalis) provide a useful conceptual framework for the analysis of Eddy's idealism. Very surprisingly, Novalis' *Notes for a Romantic Encyclopaedia* only appeared in an English translation in 2007[4] two centuries after his death, so non-German-speaking academics until recently have not had access to his 'magical idealism', a form with certain parallels to that of Eddy's idealism. Magical idealism as a form is entirely due to von Hardenberg, but sadly, owing to his premature death in 1801, a fully detailed working of this concept was never completed. However, in *Notes for a Romantic Encyclopaedia* we are provided with at least an impressionist picture of his ideas. The fact of its incompleteness, and the fragmentary character of the notes Novalis bequeathed, gives the opportunity for many interpretations regarding true intentions for his project, but some important aspects are not in doubt. Novalis' use of the word 'magical', although potentially a source of misunderstanding for twenty-first-century readers, had a very specific quasi-technical meaning at the time of Novalis' writing. He used the term to mean the capacity to cause change in an apparently external reality by the action of will, an idea relating to Novalis' equating of will and thought. However, Novalis, like Eddy 80 years later, was adamant that he did not reject rationalism, but instead sought to incorporate aesthetics into his idealism, with love being at its centre, just as McTaggart argued 120 years after Novalis' death.

---

3. Schopenhauer 1851, vol. 1, §13.
4. Novalis 1798, 1799, trans. Wood 2007.

Hegel

Hegel's absolute idealism denies the distinction between subject and object, positing this fact as a potential realisation of mind. Self-realisation advances spirit, Hegel claimed, to that of Absolute Spirit, this being prompted by the understanding that all apparently 'separate' objects are in fact 'self'. Hegel further argued that the finite man, in some ways not yet fully real, becomes infinite, attaining divine status; Hegel considered that this occurred when he first had this realisation, making *him* the culmination of all history. Although Hegel is not now believed to have quite achieved this, he is nevertheless perhaps the holder of the world record for self-aggrandisement. As Farnsworth put it in his 1909 work, *The Sophistries of Christian Science*: 'Christ was to Hegel's conception what Speculative Philosophy had realized was possible of every free ego, to wit, attained self-conscious union with God, for which the idea, even the Absolute Spirit, externalized itself as pure but characterless shadow'[5]. It is important to note that while Eddy asserted that we are all Spirit and within God, we nevertheless maintain separate identities.

The American transcendentalists

The American transcendentalists were a loose grouping of writers, clergymen and theologians who were influenced by German idealism through the interpretive texts of English and French authors, such as Taylor Coleridge, Thomas Carlyle and Victor Cousin[6]. Most had studied at either Harvard or Yale Divinity School, which in the 1820s and 1830s was surprisingly avant-garde theologically; the veracity of the Gospel accounts was a popular topic of discussion, and the historicity of all the miracles in Scripture was similarly a matter of debate. Many American transcendentalists were initially Unitarian clergymen, but as they became more strongly influenced by metaphysical idealism, a change of career beckoned; writers, educationalists and social reformers therefore ultimately dominated the movement; Ralph Waldo Emerson is the most well-known of the group, and *Nature* his best-known work. This was described by

---

5. Farnsworth 1909, pp. 108-109.
6. Grodzins 2002, p. 64.

Francis Bowen as 'philosophy in its poetical aspect'[7] and as having: 'occasional vagueness of expression, and ... a vein of mysticism that pervades the writer's whole course of thought. ... To peruse this book is often painful, the thoughts excited are frequently bewildering and the results to which they lead us, uncertain and obscure'[8].

Green, Bradley and McTaggart

Thomas Hill Green was a central member of the British idealists, whose objective idealism held that reality is monistic, but that reality transcends experience. F.H. Bradley's proposed understanding of reality was similarly monistic, but held that perception and the perceived are undifferentiated. J.M.E. McTaggart's idealism held minds and love to be the only fundamental entities, arguing impressively in *The Nature of Existence*[9] that matter, space and time are logically flawed concepts, and therefore cannot exist. McTaggart's form of idealism is particularly helpful in analysing Eddy's work, as although he published his ideas 40 to 50 years after Eddy, his detailed and carefully argued justification for his conceptual model of existence demonstrates a use of language and grasp of the rules of valid inference far beyond that of Eddy.

With regard to general works on idealism which are relevant to the analysis of Mary Baker Eddy's work, the exact opposite situation exists to that previously encountered concerning the paucity of specific works on her underlying philosophy, in that there are so many titles of books and papers on idealism that a conscious narrowing of the remit becomes essential. The subset is essentially composed of early German idealists and (with some exceptions) the later British idealists and should permit a detailed and thorough analysis.

This brief review has demonstrated the variety of material specific to Christian Science and to Mary Baker Eddy as an individual, but additionally the great choice of works available to assist with the analysis of the idealism at the heart of Christian Science. Although some serious works on the philosophy of Christian Science do exist, and have done so since at least as early as 1946, the field is still remarkably sparse. Despite the clear difficulty which this presents to any

---

7. Bowen 1836, quoted in Gura 2007, pp. 50 ff.
8. Bowen 1836 in Gura 2007, pp. 50 ff.
9. McTaggart 1921, 1927.

researcher attempting the analysis of the philosophical underpinning of Christian Science, there is nevertheless a golden cache of material of use to this purpose.

Other useful works

Attractively counterbalancing the necessarily heavy editing of the general literature on idealism is the eclectic inclusivity which may be applied to the literature pertaining to apparently non-philosophical aspects of Christian Science, and to Mary Baker Eddy's works in general. It would be a forgivable error to assume that works making false statements concerning either Mary Baker Eddy or Christian Science would be of no value to this book. Nevertheless, it would be a mistake, as surrounding the false allegations are often interesting and well-expressed points of genuine philosophical interest. What sometimes happens is that, in their enthusiasm for making critical comments, writers may go beyond their data. While this casts doubt on the overall reliability of a given work, it does not detract from other factually evidenced criticisms which they may have made.

Biographical works

Driven by its commercial expedient is the sheer quantity of literature concerning Mary Baker Eddy's life, some of which also details Christian Science; a further subset of these works also meaningfully analyse the philosophy of her creation. Although this subset is very small in relation to the totality of works in this genre, the vast number of titles in the literature as a whole means that even a minute proportion still represents a fairly large absolute number, and many of these works are of great use.

Rationale for the choice of literature

My methodology regarding the choice of material to be considered as being of use is a curious mixture of the eclectic and the highly focussed. The wide range of material concerning Mary Baker Eddy and Christian Science, and the relatively small body of work on the philosophy of Christian Science means that a catholic approach is forced upon the researcher once this subset has been defined.

However, regarding idealism, an extremely sharp focus is essential due to the sheer quantity of works available.

Conclusions and summary

The considerable notoriety which Mary Baker Eddy and Christian Science generated led to the publication of the great body of literature which is of use to this research. Although much of it is of little relevance, some is of the greatest value in assisting with the philosophical analysis of Christian Science, and so titles which at first sight may appear unhelpful nevertheless require careful and thorough reading if potentially highly valuable material is not to be missed.

This nicely segues into the next chapter, in which I will explore the idealism needed in order to analyse Christian Science's foundations. As Eddy wrote in a letter to her editor, Rev. H.J. Wiggin in 1886, 'Never change my meaning, only bring it out.' This is a perfect summarisation of what I see as the two core purposes of this book: firstly, to evince the astonishingly radical philosophical ideas which Eddy's work contains; and secondly, to demonstrate their originality. Just as many of the German idealists, Hegel in particular, wrote in a style which even other academics found impenetrably obscure, Eddy's work can be difficult for non-specialists to follow. This, in addition to the understandably negative publicity previously mentioned, has, I believe, resulted in an unjustified neglect of Eddy's work. Her profound and ingenious philosophy demands greater attention.

Chapter 6

Christian Science as a Philosophical System

Introduction

Up to this point I have outlined Eddy's theology and its underlying philosophy, but without considering either the structure of her definitive work or the text in its entirety. The focus of this chapter will be the last two of these tasks, considering the outer and inner structure of *Science and Health* and other works, and carefully editing, rephrasing or omitting Eddy's descriptions of her system of thought, thus creating a very much more concise and coherent text. This will form the source material for the philosophical analysis to come.

Beginning the re-presentation

The last edition of *Science and Health* (1910) – the 432nd – published in 1910 is considered as the definition of Christian Science by its adherents. It has the following high-level structure:

> Preface
> Chapter 1 Prayer
> Chapter 2 Atonement and Eucharist
> Chapter 3 Marriage
> Chapter 4 Christian Science versus Spiritualism

Chapter 5 Animal Magnetism Unmasked
Chapter 6 Science, Theology, Medicine
Chapter 7 Physiology
Chapter 8 Footsteps of Truth
Chapter 9 Creation
Chapter 10 Science of Being
Chapter 11 Some Objections Answered
Chapter 12 Christian Science Practice
Chapter 13 Teaching Christian Science
Chapter 14 Recapitulation
Chapter 15 Genesis
Chapter 16 The apocalypse
Chapter 17 Glossary
Chapter 18 Fruitage (testimonials from patients etc.)

All of these chapters have what are effectively section titles, even though they are printed as marginalia, and these could provide names for the fragments of text which will either form part of the re-expressed description of Eddy's system of belief, or be excluded on various grounds. Some fragments will fall outside her argument, being extraneous to its logical progression, but the modal reason for exclusion is simply the repetition of a pre-existing stage of her deductive process.

A recapping of Eddy's system may be helpful in understanding the nature of the analysis which this chapter will present. Eddy begins with three statements which are at this stage effectively axioms of her system:

1. 'God is All-in-all.'
2. 'God is good.'
3. 'God is Mind.'

Following these she immediately deduces that everything, without exception, must be good. Eddy then goes on to conclude that humans are the perfect spiritual ideas of a single, divine Mind, and are composed of Spirit, not material substance. What are conventionally thought of as the five physical senses, on the basis that they do not provide information concerning Spirit, are therefore in reality misleading, and are responsible for the almost universally held 'false beliefs' regarding the existence of pain, illness, disability, death etc. Eddy, having concluded that all sickness is simply an error of belief, reasoned that praying in the company of the patient on this issue could dispel the belief and result in the disappearance of the supposed illness. This is expressed in *Science and Health* as follows as the 'scientific statement of being':

> There is no life, truth, intelligence, nor substance in matter. All is infinite Mind and its infinite manifestation, for God is All-in-all. Spirit is immortal Truth; matter is mortal error. Spirit is the real and eternal; matter is the unreal and temporal. Spirit is God, and man is His image and likeness. Therefore man is not material; he is spiritual.[1]

For Eddy, the disappearance of the previous symptoms provided the third element in the sequence of hypothesis, experiment, results and conclusion, wherein the hypothesis is (at present) the set of three axioms, and the experiment is the attempt at 'healing' the patient by prayer. Eddy considered that any improvement in the patient's apparent condition confirmed the hypotheses; this approach to metaphysics she therefore claimed to be scientific, as it was, from her point of view, following scientific method. Each incidence of a 'cure' thus added weight to the veracity of her initial assumptions, ultimately to the point where Eddy could revise the three initial statements not as axioms, but, in her view, as hypotheses which she had experimentally demonstrated.

An extremely important and fundamental difference between what Eddy suggested and Berkeley's form of idealism rests upon Eddy's understanding of what is normally considered as being our physical senses. All the way through her many prose works are references to, and explanations of, these so-called senses being in reality generators of error – of false beliefs. For Eddy, only what she termed our 'spiritual sense' is capable of providing meaningful information. The consequence of this reframing of the 'five senses' is that, whereas Berkeley was subtly redefining the nature of reality, not its existence, Eddy on the other hand denied both its existence and even its possibility of existence. Although a radical step, it neatly

---

1. Eddy 1910, p. 468.

circumvents many of the difficulties which Berkeley's approach creates, including some of those of which Berkeley was himself aware and mentioned in his works.

Berkeley's suggestion that the continued existence of his claimed version of reality is maintained by God's awareness of it – something which if adopted creates a multitude of problems itself – was not needed by Eddy, for whom everything which exists is within God, due to the elegantly simple reason that God and the divine thought of God is everything. It is worth re-emphasising a very important aspect relating to this idea, as it has been the subject of a persistent misunderstanding regarding Christian Science and pantheism; Christian Science is emphatically not pantheistic, despite the statement above. This is because a vital distinction exists between pantheism and panentheism; the former can be summarised as 'God is within everything', whereas the latter implies that 'everything is within God'. These two statements, which can sound very similar to some readers, are in reality conveying completely different concepts.

The approach to the analysis

Paraphrasing Gottschalk, it has been stated[2] that Eddy's approach to *Science and Health* created the situation in which the sentences making up its content had no particular reason for being in the position or order in which they were published. Given that Eddy considered her work as 'revealed truth', this is unsurprising; she believed God to be the authority for her beliefs, so a coherent argument consisting of a logical sequence of deductions following from her initial premises was not her highest priority, especially as she considered the occasional genuine 'cures' of her patients as empirical proof of her beliefs. It does, however, greatly add to the effort involved in this analysis of her work.

The process of rephrasing and editing Eddy's original prose could be a complex one, involving several stages:

1. Classifying the content of each of the 1274 named sections in *Science and Health*;

---

2. Gottschalk 2006, p. 43.

2. Producing a minimal subset of those sections sufficient to fully describe Eddy's philosophical system, but minimising redundancy; and
3. Rephrasing the content of sections in the chosen subset.

The original text consists of 1274 sections with an average of about 160 words each, so even if it were re-expressed as a subset of just 100, it would still represent a total wordcount of 16,000 or so, which is unwieldy given that the whole point of providing a shorter expression of Eddy's text is to facilitate the discovery and analysis of idealism within her work. Consequently, rephrasing the text in some other manner is vital, not simply clarifying Eddy's sometimes obscure expression, but distilling it to point of 'conceptual purity', where only the ideas remain.

The presentation

Although the approach described above would be achievable in principle, due to the nature of Eddy's writing it would be an impractically slow and cumbersome procedure, and despite *Science and Health* being what she saw as a complete statement of Christian Science, it would miss out some aspects which are important to the analysis of her work interpreted as idealist philosophy. Thankfully, there is a very much better way, which is to use a subset from *Science and Health* augmented by material from Eddy's shorter works, and it is this alternative methodology which will be adopted.

Two observations which are almost unavoidable from the process of editing and rephrasing Eddy's work are that, firstly, it develops over time with regard to its complexity and coherency, and, secondly, there is no reduction in redundancy – if anything, it increases. Both these points are of importance: an increase in coherency over time suggests, very strongly, that what Eddy was creating was her own work, as opposed to revealed truth; and secondly, the unreduced redundancy in her writing, with many conceptual aspects being repeated very many times, appears to imply the same aspect. Unfortunately, the Christian Science Church has not yet digitised all the editions of *Science and Health*, but certain key editions, where changes of significance have occurred, are available. The editions are the first, the last and a rapidly increasing number of others. In each case, changes or additions have qualitatively altered the conceptual content of the work.

The chosen subset of sections from *Science and Health*, which I believe represents a first step in the succinct expression of Eddy's system of thought, reveals the unexpected finding that many are composed of a combination of separate themes or elements within her philosophical system.

There are a number of terms needing definitions before embarking upon the process of choosing a subset of Eddy's sections, restructuring them and rephrasing their content. Additionally, I will distinguish between Eddy's core argument, a more elaborated version which I will term Eddy's main argument, and finally the longer description of the philosophy underpinning Christian Science's theology, which I will call Eddy's philosophical system.

As I have previously stated, it has been observed that individual sentences in *Science and Health* do not have 'a particular reason for being where they are'[3]; perhaps surprisingly, this affords the researcher a curious and unexpected advantage: the 'decomposition' of her work can extend below the level of the sections to that of the individual sentences within them, permitting a much greater degree of restructuring of Eddy's original text, as sentences expressing the same idea can be re-grouped as newly formed sections where this helps bring out her meaning. This will assist in the levels of restructuring, as each section of the new text will be more sharply focussed on a specific concept or concepts, rather than being diluted by extraneous material.

Regarding Eddy's original source material, how, then, are we to reconcile the idea that the physical universe simply doesn't exist with the reliance on the Bible – presumably a physically existent one – as an essential part of Eddy's argument against the existence of physical universe? This is the first of three major problems with Eddy's system which require solutions for it to stand. The answer, which is so important in establishing the coherency of Christian Science, depends entirely on Eddy's understanding of the so-called physical senses as generators not of information about a hypothetical external physical reality, but as creators of illusory ideas, i.e. of falsehoods. All throughout her many works, Eddy clearly emphasises not merely the

---

3. Gottschalk 1973, p. 43.

pre-eminence of spiritual sense, but that it is the only true sense, i.e. providing information about reality – spiritual reality. For the Bible to be (i) existent, (ii) true and (iii) interrogatable by spiritual sense in Eddy's meaning of the phrase, it must therefore be a spiritual entity and present to the spiritual sense. Given that Eddy considered it as an absolutely error-free source of information about the nature and attributes of God and of his creation, and that God is purely Spirit, it is not unreasonable for the form in which this uniquely important information is presented to also be entirely spiritual.

As the entire focus of this book is upon Eddy's thought, it follows that giving her the benefit of the doubt on matters relating to apparent contradictions is a reasonable initial position to take, for if I did not believe her system to be worthy of serious analysis it would not form the basis for this book. What follows, therefore, will be an analysis predicated upon the general principle that Eddy is aware of the logical consequences of her sometimes highly polemic assertions, whether taken individually, as a subset or in their entirety. If this ultimately reveals unavoidable inconsistency in either her philosophical arguments or conclusions resulting from them, then I will treat these observations as the answer to the question with which this work begins. Eddy's many critics, often highly vocal, widely published and even at times litigious, raised many questions about her system of thought, pointing out what they believed to be self-evident inconsistencies. Eddy was at least equally keen to publish replies to what she saw as false criticisms; having a publishing company at her disposal facilitated her in this regard. Many of Eddy's shorter works address these issues explicitly, consisting of a series of questions focussed upon centrally important assertions and especially those which appear to be either self-contradictory or contradict other aspects of Christian Science.

A problem facing any scholar seeking to establish a consistent understanding of the philosophy underlying Eddy's system of thought is her highly variable approach to the veracity (or otherwise) of what is conventionally thought of as physical reality. Although her theoretical approach eschews it completely, certain aspects of her writing appear to reference its existence. I believe that a consistent pattern exists to this vitally important component of her thought, and it is Gottschalk's failure to discern it, as opposed to Steiger's perception of it (albeit only partially), which accounts for the difference in their conclusions regarding this aspect. Although Eddy occasionally uses the language of physical reality, it is purely a *metaphor* for the spiritual truth of the concept under consideration. She herself effectively makes this point in a published answer to a question from a member of her Church, and this will be explored in detail later.

The core argument

Four of Eddy's shortest works – *Unity of Good, Rudimental Divine Science, Christian Science versus Pantheism* and *The People's Idea of God* – provide a small set of axioms which form the core of her ideas. These are largely expressed using a printed version of the dialogue-based Socratic method, with both the questions and the answers on a small number of central topics. These can be rephrased so as to avoid the question-and-answer format, thereby forming the kernel of her system, and creating the foundation upon which the main argument, and ultimately the complete philosophical system, can be constructed. At this stage, the core axioms are precisely that – axiomatic – but later in this book they will have been demonstrated empirically in the manner which Eddy considered sufficiently robust for her to assume their validity to have been proved.

The main argument

The main argument consists of a much larger set of corollaries and a handful of lesser, extra principles taken from Eddy's second-most important work, *Miscellaneous Writings* (Eddy 1897), where they are again expressed using a form of the Socratic method.

Although completing the formal component of Eddy's system, the main argument does not complete the system as a whole. Completion requires 'closing the loop' with empirical evidence in support of her claims, and a very detailed discussion regarding the concept known as 'science'.

The philosophical system

Eddy's philosophical system as re-expressed therefore consists of the set of principles formed by the core and main arguments, an examination of what constitutes 'science' and what is needed in order to permit a 'theological science' to be constructed, and a vast (and continually growing) body of empirical evidence consisting of the testimonies of patients and their attending physicians. Thankfully, although this catalogue of evidence had already grown to two million examples by the 1890s, only a minimal, necessary subset of those testimonies is required in order to corroborate the main argument. Instead, it is the discussion of the concept of 'science' and the efforts of MacIntosh[4], Torrance[5] and Polkinghorne[6] which will become a large and important component of the section completing Eddy's system.

Inherent difficulties

There is a second, very important difficulty regarding Eddy's work for which it is absolutely essential to find a method of resolution if her system is to be coherent. Eddy's understanding of the word 'infinite' echoes that of Spinoza two centuries before her, in that she interprets it as meaning 'everything', as opposed 'going on for ever'. I believe that an argument composed of ideas from the branch of mathematics which relates to transfinite numbers, in combination with an intriguing and possibly novel application of apophatic theology, addresses this difficulty. In *Science and Health* Eddy provides three main definitions of the Christian Science understanding of God, presented in a question-and-answer format and which I quote in full below. At this point it may be important to remind the reader that the nebulousness and incoherency which they are about to meet in Eddy's original text is precisely what I am seeking to remove, substituting a new presentation of her system in a hopefully clearer and more appropriate form:

> *Definition 1.* 'Q. What is God? A. God is incorporeal, divine, supreme, infinite Mind, Spirit, Soul, Principle, Life, Truth, Love. Q Are these terms synonymous? A. They are. They refer to one absolute God. They are also intended to express the nature, essence and wholeness of Deity. The attributes of God are justice, mercy, wisdom, goodness and so on. Q. Is there more than one God or Principle? A . There is not. Principle and its idea is one, and

---

4. MacIntosh 1919.
5. Torrance 1969.
6. Polkinghorne 1988.

Christian Science as a Philosophical System

this one is God, omnipotent, omniscient and omnipresent Being, and His reflection is man and the universe. *omni* is adopted from the Latin adjective meaning *all*. Hence God combines all power or potency, all science or true knowledge all presence. The varied manifestations of Christian Science indicate Mind, never mind matter, and have one principle.'[7]

The next definition is from the Glossary in *Science and Health*:

Definition 2. 'GOD: The great I AM; the all-knowing, all-seeing, all-acting, all-wise, all-loving, and eternal; Principle; Mind; Soul; Spirit; Life; Truth; Love all substance; intelligence.'[8]

The third definition occurs in Chapter 10 of *Science and Health*:

Definition 3. The Deific Supremacy 'God is infinite, the only Life, substance, Spirit, or Soul, the only intelligence of the universe, including man. Eye hath neither seen God nor His image and likeness. Neither God nor the perfect man can be discerned by the material senses. The individuality of Spirit, or the infinite, is unknown, and thus a knowledge of it is left to human conjecture or revelation of divine Science.'[9]

In Christian Science the word 'man' does not refer to the (apparently) physical form of a human being, which Eddy describes as the empirical concept. Again, this can be extremely misleading, as, far from an objectively real presence, she is distinguishing between this unreal, purely conjectural, erroneous concept and the true, spiritual reality, for which she offers the following definition:

Man is not matter, he is not made up of brain, blood, bones and other material elements. The Scriptures inform us that

---

7. Eddy 1910, pp. 465-66.
8. Ibid., p. 587.
9. Ibid., p. 330.

man is made in the image and likeness of God. Matter is not that likeness. The likeness of Spirit cannot be so unlike Spirit.[10]

Eddy then goes on to distinguish 'metaphysical man' from 'empirical man':

Man is spiritual and perfect; and because he is spiritual and perfect, he must be so understood in Christian Science. Man is idea, the image, of Love; he is not physique [sic]. He is the compound idea of God, including all right ideas; the generic term for all that reflects God's image and likeness; the conscious identity of being as found in Science [by which Eddy of course means Christian Science], in which man is the reflection of God, or Mind, and therefore is eternal.[11]

As Steiger put it[12] 'Man lives as God's image and likeness. God is the Mind, man the effect of Mind. As quoted in the definition of man, God is principle, and man the idea.'

The concept of mortal mind

Eddy (1910, p. 103) gives the following definition of the concept of mortal mind and is careful to distinguish it from the idea of immortal Mind:

It is the false belief that mind is in matter, and is both evil and good; that evil is as real as good and more powerful. … It is either ignorant or malicious… The truths of immortal mind sustain man, and they annihilate the fables of mortal mind, whose flimsy and gaudy pretensions, like silly moths, singe their own wings and fall into dust.

---

10. Ibid., p. 475.
11. Ibid., p. 475.
12. Steiger 1946, p. 68.

Earlier in the same work Eddy describes God as 'immortal Mind' and 'that which [imagines that it] sins, suffers and dies' as '*mortal* mind'[13].

Interestingly, F.H. Bradley arrived at something broadly similar, although with a different terminology. He conceived reality in terms of a monistic whole in which is there is no difference between perception and that which is perceived; he held that nothing can exist unless it is known by a mind:

> This is the point on which I insist... I mean that to be real is to be indissolubly one thing with sentience. ... What I repudiate is the separation of feeling from the felt, or of the desired from the desire, or what is thought from thinking, or... of anything from anything from anything else.[14]

He explains this further with a rather curious choice of language:

> For if, seeking for reality we go to experience, what we certainly do *not* find [italics in the original] is a subject, or an object, or indeed any other thing, standing separate and on its own bottom.[15]

So Eddy's assertion is 'that mind is a quality of God'[16]. She acknowledges that the term 'mortal mind' is self-contradictory, but suggests that it is nevertheless necessary as an intermediate step in the process of correcting the errors of naïve realism. Basing one's own model of reality on the idea of an external world and one's physical existence in that world allows contrary explanations to be dismissed as inconsistent, but once one's real-world model has become metaphysical, then the coherency of an external spiritual existence (remembering that in Eddy's world view, Spirit occupies space) and the unreality of the 'physical world' becomes apparent; 'The dream and the dreamer are one'[17].

---

13. Eddy 1910, p. 25.
14. Bradley 1893, p. 146.
15. Ibid., p. 146.
16. Steiger 1946, p. 90.
17. Eddy 1910, p. 530.

Mortal mind, the Ptolemaic model and phlogiston

The concept of mortal mind is also analogous with the Ptolemaic model of the solar system[18], which wrongly placed the earth at its centre, and required a multiplicity of increasingly complex (wholly fictitious) artificial epicycles in order to achieve a reasonable degree of computational accuracy. Similarly, the idea of mortal mind wrongly places this construct as subject at the conceptual centre of the universe, all of which is then regarded as object. Regarding mortal mind as merely a hypothesis, however, allows the possibility of an alternative model, in which human existence is metaphysical and a reflection of the universe; an object, as opposed to a subject. A similar and perhaps better analogy can be drawn between the hypothetical substance 'phlogiston' and the concept of 'mortal mind'. Phlogiston was suggested by eighteenth-century chemists as a flammable 'essence' which all combustible substances must contain, and which was used up in the process of combustion. A better understanding of the process, however, demonstrated that combustion was a process of combining substances – the flammable material and the oxygen in air – rather than one of elimination. Similarly, 'mortal mind' is merely a hypothetical construct created to explain the apparent existence of human intelligence. Once seen as a consequence of the divine Mind, the idea of 'mortal mind' is no longer needed. The Christian Science concept of 'divine Mind' is analogous to both the Greek idea of nous and the Hegelian concept of Absolute Mind. In answer to the question 'who or what is it that believes?' Eddy explained that:

> Spirit is all-knowing; this precludes the need for believing. Matter cannot believe, and Mind understands… Christian evidence is founded on Science or demonstrable truth, flowing from immortal mind, and there is no such thing in reality as mortal mind.[19]

Here Eddy is implying that mortal mind does not refer to an existing entity, and is simply part of an erroneous model of reality. Based on the concept that the true essence or existence of man 'is not mortal or

---

18. Steiger 1946, p. 95.
19. Eddy 1910, p. 487.

limited'[20], mortal mind vanishes, along with the similarly erroneous belief in the reality of evil; both this belief and any question as to the origin of evil also vanish. As Gottschalk explains, 'the unreality of evil can be known to us only as we put on the Mind of Christ. As one follows in Jesus' way actually dissolving all forms of evil in his experience, he knows and understands the unreality of evil… The understanding… therefore, is inseparable from its demonstration'[21]. For Eddy, salvation was not quite as mainstream theology imagined it. Instead of it being centred on Christ as mediator between God and mankind, with salvation being due to the grace of God, Eddy defined it as the realisation that the 'complete elimination of mortal mind' is required in order to yield a coherent metaphysical system[22]. However, as virtually the entirety of those new to Christian Science will, as foundation, rely on 'common-sense naïve realism', the self-contradictory term 'mortal mind' is needed as an artifice to help with the transition to a metaphysical understanding of the nature of Mind.

Eddy's descriptions of Christian Science

Although *Science and Health* (Eddy 1910) is definitive with regard to Christian Science, Eddy wrote many other works which serve as an introduction or clarification of her 700-page 'textbook'. It is these shorter books which will now be considered.

In addition to her primary work, *Science and Health with Key to the Scriptures*, and some autobiographical reflections, Mary Baker Eddy wrote and published many other works during her lifetime, including the following texts: *Rudimental Divine Science*[23] answers some of the most commonly asked questions about Christian Science and how it heals. *Unity of Good*[24] provides a better understanding of how God as completely good can bring healing to one's life. Fifteen short, individual chapters address subjects such as 'The Ego', 'Soul' and 'The Deep Things of God'. *Christian Science versus Pantheism*[25] defends (with an unusual degree of logic) Eddy's system of thought from

---

20. Gottschalk 1973, p. 67.
21. Gottschalk 1973, p. 67.
22. Steiger 1946, p. 97.
23. Eddy 1891b; 17 pages.
24. Eddy 1891; 64 pages.
25. Eddy 1898; 15 pages.

accusations of pantheism and discusses how pantheistic beliefs have no relation to the concept of one universal God caring for man. *No and Yes*[26] is a thought-provoking look at Christian Science in relation to other Christian faith traditions. In *Miscellaneous Writings 1883-1896*[27] Eddy produced a collection of writings which she believed so important that in 1897 she requested that students of her ideas spend the next year thoroughly reading it. The diverse articles, addresses, letters and poems – on topics such as mental healing, forgiveness, angels and marriage – are based on the author's own experiences in putting her system of healing into practice. Considered by Eddy to be a book that would help readers better understand *Science and Health*, it contains dozens of letters from people healed just by reading that work. *Retrospection and Introspection*[28] is a short, reflective work on Eddy's life and work up to the point of publication. Some more of Eddy's individually published texts are also very short: in *Christian Healing*[29] Mary Baker Eddy explains how the healings performed by Jesus and his early followers are possible today; *The People's Idea of God – Its Effect on Health and Christianity*[30] looks at how individuals' lives are influenced by their views of God, and the life-transforming effect of spiritual ideas; *Message to the Mother Church for 1900*[31] includes a discussion of the 'right thinker and worker', obedience to God and love for mankind; in *Message to the Mother Church for 1901*[32] Eddy addresses the Church on the topics 'Christ is One and Divine', My Childhood's Church Home', and 'Medicine'; and in *Message to the Mother Church for 1902*[33], she focusses on the First Commandment and Jesus' commandment to 'love one another'.

Eddy's clarity of expression and logical progression of argument appears to be in inverse proportion to the length of her writing. As a consequence, in addition to Chapter 14 of *Science and Health*, I will use four of her very short works and a single chapter from her two longest ones; the complete set of source documents is therefore as

---

26. Eddy 1891a; 46 pages.
27. Eddy 1897; 471 pages.
28. Eddy 1891, 1892; 95 pages.
29. Eddy 1883; 20 pages.
30. Eddy 1883; 14 pages.
31. Eddy 1900; 15 pages.
32. Eddy 1901; 35 pages.
33. Eddy 1902; 20 pages.

follows: Chapter 14 of *Science and Health* ; *Rudimental Divine Science, No and Yes, Unity of Good, Christian Science versus Pantheism*, and Chapter 3 of *Miscellaneous Writings 1883-1896*.

Summary

Due to the careful selection of a representative subset of Eddy's writing, and the brevity of Eddy's core argument, her curious disdain for logical progression in communicating the concepts within Christian Science is less apparent within the chosen sections of her works. Comparatively little re-ordering or re-expression of the fundamental axioms of the core argument is therefore necessary. Although Eddy considered Christian Science as revealed truth, potentially justifying the manner in which she herself understood its ideas, it does not explain why she had a clear tendency to retain this un-sequenced approach when attempting to communicate the ideas to others, and especially so in the case of her paying students. Viewed en masse, her approach can be thought of as 'endlessly' repeating a relatively small set of principles, using differently worded statements to express them in an almost entirely random sequence; the phrase reductio ad nauseam comes to mind.

The focus now moves to setting forth the foundational principles of Christian Science. Eddy's Christian Science begins with five initially axiomatic principles:

> Core Axiom 1. God is omniscient.
> Core Axiom 2. God is omnipotent.
> Core Axiom 3. God is omnipresent.
> Core Axiom 4. God is infinite.
> Core Axiom 5. God is (completely/infinitely) good.

From these Eddy makes a number of deductions, most of which form the augmentation to the core argument, but some of which are within what I define as the core. First and foremost is her deduction that, as God is infinite (which she interprets as meaning 'without limit', which she further interprets as implying 'is everything') , and God is good, then it follows that everything – absolutely everything – must be good [Main Argument 1]. This is how she determines at the outset of her system that pain, illness and death cannot possibly be real [Main Argument 2], from which it follows that our 'physical senses' must be nothing of the sort [Main Argument 3], and that we must therefore rely entirely on our spiritual sense [Main Argument 4] coupled with logical deduction. The core argument and the first four deductions arising from it, despite their fundamental importance, form only the very first step in setting forth the nuanced, highly complex and original system which Christian Science represents. By far the greatest part of the threefold presentation adopted by this book will appear as the development of the main argument, with the empirical 'proof' second in length. Consequently, if Eddy's argument appears simplistic or contradictory at this stage, it is not the fault of Eddy; concerns such as these will be addressed later in this work.

In conclusion

As is very often the case when reading Eddy's many works, and particularly when attempting to analyse them, one is faced with the twin difficulties of her sometimes counterintuitive use of language and her seemingly random ordering of the concepts being expressed. Whereas the latter can merely lead to a lack of comprehension, the former can create serious misunderstandings, even to the point of the reader assuming the diametrical opposite to the meaning Eddy intended to convey.

The next chapter presents an analysis of the internal consistency of Eddy's system of thought.

Chapter 7

Christian Science Reframed

To recap, the main argument consists of the core axioms and the deductions Eddy made from them. In her original text, these are not always made explicitly, instead sometimes being the implications of answers to questions she received from her many readers and published as part of one of her shorter works. Even during her lifetime, sales of her books were in the region of one million copies, and because of their content and style, this naturally encouraged curious readers to write to her for clarifications, either due to the highly counterintuitive conceptual material, or as a result of the variable clarity of its presentation.

Apparent inconsistencies in Eddy's work will be treated as precisely that – apparent rather than real. Given the near half-century of thought she devoted to Christian Science, and the extraordinary 432 editions of *Science and Health*, quite apart from her multitude of other works, it would be reasonable to make the assumption of consistency on this basis alone. However, for the purpose of this analysis, the 'meta-axiom' initially adopted is that Eddy's axioms, corollaries and other statements do not contradict one another. In the same manner that Eddy's own axioms are ultimately demonstrated empirically (or, at least, deductions following from empirical results do so to Eddy's satisfaction), I aim to demonstrate that apparently contradictory aspects to Christian Science can be resolved at a later stage.

Eddy's idiosyncratic use of words in everyday usage and of terms from conventional theology could lead to a degree of misapprehension completely undermining the intelligibility of her main argument, and, by extension, her philosophical system. Consequently, although a full glossary is included as an appendix after the main body of this book, a discussion of a brief but targeted lexicon is necessary as the analysis progresses.

Having expressed the core of Eddy's Christian Science as a small set of (temporarily) axiomatic principles, the presentation of her argument moves on to a far more elaborate structure. Although built upon the foundation already provided, the first part of this new stage relies on a qualitatively different mode of presentation consisting of an edited, but nevertheless quite substantial, set of questions and answers regarding Christian Science drawn from Eddy's own work. I have used the very short texts *Rudimental Divine Science, No and Yes, Christian Science versus Pantheism* and *The Unity of Good*, in combination with passages from Chapter 3 of *Miscellaneous Writings 1883-1896*. Although Chapters 10 and 14 of Eddy's longest work, *Science and Health*, are of relevance, they will, however, be more helpful in the later, analytical chapters of the book. The second part of expressing the main argument involves rewording the questions and answers as an exposition of the principles of Christian Science.

The next series of quotes is exceptionally important:

> According to Christian Science, the first idolatrous claim of sin is, that matter exists; the second, that matter is substance; the third, that matter has intelligence; and the fourth, that matter, being so endowed, produces life and death. Hence my conscientious position, in the denial of matter.[1]

> Spirit is the only creator, and man, including the universe, is His spiritual concept. By matter is commonly meant mind, – not the highest Mind, but a false form of mind. This so-called mind and matter cannot be separated in origin and action. What is this mind?[2]

> Sight: Mortal mind declares that matter sees through the organizations of matter, or that mind sees by means of

---

1. Eddy 1888, p. 31.
2. Ibid., p. 32.

> matter... that God is All, and God is Spirit; therefore there is nothing but Spirit; and consequently there is no matter. Touch. Take another train of reasoning. Mortal mind says that matter cannot feel matter... What evidence does mortal mind afford that matter is substantial, is hot or cold? Take away mortal mind, and matter could not feel what it calls 'substance'. Take away matter, and mortal mind could not cognize its own so-called substance, and this so-called mind would have no identity. ... What is substance? What is the reality of God and the universe? Immortal Mind is the real substance, – Spirit, Life, Truth, and Love. Taste: Mortal mind says, 'I taste; and this is sweet, this is sour.' Let mortal mind change, and say that sour is sweet, and *so* it would be. If every mortal mind believed sweet to be sour, it would be so; for the qualities of matter are but qualities of mortal mind. Change the mind, and the quality changes. Destroy the belief, and the quality disappears.[3]

Here, Eddy is providing her argument for the radically idealist world model which underpins Christian Science. She is seeking to demonstrate that every aspect of what is considered by others to be caused by interactions with an external world is merely a belief, and that it many cases – perhaps even most of them – it is simply wrong; a false belief. For Eddy, the only reality is God. Eddy then addresses some highly important specific questions as described in the next section.

Selected passages from *No and Yes* (Eddy 1887)

Eddy addressed further questions in this fairly short yet very helpful work *No and Yes*.

> Is Christian Science blasphemous? Blasphemy has never diminished sin or sickness, nor acknowledged God in all His ways. Blasphemy rebukes not the godless lie that denies Him as All-in-all, nor does it ascribe to Him all presence, power, and glory. Christian Science does this.[4]

---

3. Ibid., p. 33-35.
4. Eddy 1887a, p. 18.

Eddy then continues with an important deduction:

> Is there a personal devil? No man hath seen the person of good or of evil. Each is greater than the corporeality we behold. 'He cast out *devils.*' This record shows that the term devil is generic, being used in the plural number. From this it follows that there is more than one devil. That Jesus cast several persons out of another person, is not stated, and is impossible. Hence the passage must refer to the *evils* [by which Eddy means 'errors' or 'lies'] which were cast out.[5]

At this point Eddy first mentions Spinoza, which is important to the analysis later.

> According to Spinoza's philosophy God is amplification. He is in all things, and therefore He is in evil in human thought. He is extension, of whatever character. Also, according to Spinoza, man is an animal vegetable, developed through the lower orders of matter and mortal mind. All these vagaries are at variance with my system of metaphysics, which rests on God as One and All, and denies the actual existence of both matter and evil.[6]

Shortly afterwards, Eddy offers this summary:

> Mortal man has but a false sense of Soul and body. He believes that Spirit, or Soul, exists in matter. This is pantheism, and is not the Science of Soul.[7]

Selected text from *Miscellaneous Writing 1883-1896* (Eddy 1897)

Amongst much else in this longer text, Eddy focusses on a commonly asked question, especially so in the nineteenth century:

---

5. Eddy 1887a, p. 22.
6. Eddy 1887a, p. 24.
7. Ibid., p. 29.

> If I have the toothache, and nothing stops it until I have the tooth extracted, and then the pain ceases, has the mind, or extracting, or both, caused the pain to cease? What you thought was pain in the bone or nerve, could only have been a belief in pain in matter, for matter has no sensation. It was a state of mortal thought made manifest in the flesh. You call this body matter, when awake, or when asleep in a dream. That matter can report pain, or that mind is *in* matter, reporting sensations, is but a dream at all times. You believed that if the tooth were extracted, the pain would cease: this demand of mortal thought once met, your belief assumed a new form, and said, There is no more pain. When your belief in pain ceases, the pain stops.[8]

This analysis was particularly in evidence during the 1918-19 Spanish Influenza pandemic, when it was central to the Christian Science Church's understanding of what was taking place. Self-evidently, this is of great relevance to the COVID-19 pandemic. The next question answered below is a surprising but nevertheless genuine reader's enquiry: 'Was ever a person made insane by studying metaphysics? Such an occurrence would be impossible, for the proper study of Mind-healing would cure the insane'[9]. So even if one was apparently driven insane by such radical idealism – 'apparently', because as all illness does not exist, psychiatric illness, as a subset, also cannot exist – it would also provide the healing, as the insanity would be a delusion: a delusion that one was insane. But the presence of a delusion is one of a range of possible symptoms of a psychotic illness, so this appears to create a paradox; it is analogous to a hypochondriac worrying that they have hypochondria!

The following question concerns one of the potentially serious flaws in Eddy's system (which will be considered in greater detail later). 'How does Mrs. Eddy know that she has read and studied correctly, if one must deny the evidences [sic] of the senses? She had to use her eyes to read'[10]. Eddy provided this answer:

> Jesus said, 'Having eyes, see ye not?' I read the inspired page through a higher than mortal sense. As matter, the eye

---

8. Eddy 1897, p. 44.
9. Eddy 1897, p. 48.
10. Eddy 1897, p. 58.

cannot see; and as mortal mind, it is a belief that sees. I may read the Scriptures through a belief of eyesight; but I must spiritually understand them to interpret their Science.[11]

In Christian Science, the partial isomorphism between illusory physical reality and true spiritual reality is a highly variable one, but could be explained, within Eddy's system, as being due to a limitation of our very early stage in developing spiritual sense. The next question posits an interesting concept: if we cannot believe the evidence of our eyes, would it not permit the possibility of their being far more (or far fewer) real minds than there are false bodies?

> If mortal mind and body are myths, what is the connection between them and real identity, and why are there as many identities as mortal bodies? Every material belief hints the existence of spiritual reality. ... The education of the future will be instruction, in spiritual Science, against the material... counterfeit sciences. All... will be swallowed up by the reality and omnipotence of Truth over error, and of Life over death.[12]

Eddy also considers the 'nature versus nurture' debate: 'Does Christian Science set aside the law of transmission, prenatal desires, and good or bad influences on the unborn child?'[13]. Here, Eddy is being asked about heritability, which at the time of her writing was almost universally believed to be not merely important, but, by many academics in biology and psychology, of sole importance. Her answer is that it does not occur at all:

> Whatever is humanly conceived is a departure from divine law; hence its mythical origin and certain end. According to the Scriptures, – St. Paul declares astutely, 'For of Him, and through Him, and to Him, are all things,' – man is incapable of originating; nothing can be formed apart from God, good, the all-knowing Mind. What seems to be of human origin is the counterfeit of the divine.[14]

---

11. Ibid., p. 58.
12. Ibid., pp. 60-61.
13. Eddy 1897, p. 71.
14. Ibid., p. 71.

This (the denial of inherited characteristics) is something claimed decades later in 1913 by John Broadus Watson in his so-called 'Behaviorist Manifesto'. Watson's paper, 'Psychology as the Behaviorist Views It'[15], triggered a revolution in psychology, eschewing introspection, mental states and the inheritance of characteristics, while promoting the influence of environment and the necessity of quantifiable, objective data. This last point is another curious point of similarity between Watson and Eddy, despite Watson's rigorous materialism and Eddy's radical idealism, in that it was the objective, measurable recovery of her patients that Eddy cited as both evidence for the truth of her ideas and, crucially, the validity of her methodology.

Selected text from *Christian Science versus Pantheism* (Eddy 1898)

Eddy regarded mainstream Christianity as having pantheistic tendencies, which she vehemently abjured, and was consequently angered by what she saw as the wholly unjust criticism that Christian Science was pantheistic. Her published response on this topic formed this short book, in which she explained her position in some detail. As this is such an important aspect of her system, revisiting this topic with a fairly lengthy set of quotes is needed in order to do Eddy justice:

> The Standard Dictionary has it that pantheism is the doctrine of the deification of natural causes, conceived as one personified nature, to which the religious sentiment is directed.[16]

> Theism is the belief in the personality and infinite mind of one supreme, holy, self-existent God, who reveals Himself supernaturally to His creation.[17]

> It is the doctrine that the universe owes its origin and continuity to the reason, intellect, and will of a self-existent

---

15. Watson 1913.
16. Eddy 1898, p. 2.
17. Ibid., p. 3.

> divine Being, who possesses all wisdom, goodness, and power, and is the creator and preserver of man.[18]

> Christianity, as taught and demonstrated in the first century by our great Master, virtually annulled the so-called laws of matter, idolatry, pantheism, and polytheism.[19]

> The doctrines that embrace pantheism, polytheism, and paganism are admixtures of matter and Spirit, truth and error, sickness and sin, life and death.[20]

They constantly reiterate the belief of pantheism, that mind 'sleeps in the mineral, dreams in the animal, and wakes in man'[21].

> From a material standpoint, the best of people sometimes object to the philosophy of Christian Science, on the ground that it takes away man's personality and makes man less than man. But what saith the apostle? – even this: 'If a man think himself to be something, when he is nothing, he deceiveth himself.' The great Nazarene Prophet said, 'By their fruits ye shall know them:' then, if the effects of Christian Science on the lives of men be thus judged, we are sure the honest verdict of humanity will attest its uplifting power, and prevail over the opposite notion that Christian Science lessens man's individuality.[22]

Again, it is Eddy's empiricism which is such an original aspect of her ideas.

Limitations

As stated earlier, certain essential aspects of Christian Science are highly problematic; this is now the point at which a resolution of these difficulties must be found if a coherent second philosophical system is

---

18. Ibid., p. 4.
19. Ibid., p. 8.
20. Ibid., p. 8.
21. Eddy 1898, pp. 9, 10.
22. Ibid., pp. 9, 10.

to be achievable. To restate the problem, Eddy uses the word 'infinite' to mean 'everything', as opposed to 'going on for ever'. Spinoza made the same interpretation, to which the classical rejoinder is to offer for consideration the set of all even numbers; it is clearly infinite, as it goes on for ever, but it is equally self-evidently not everything, as it by definition it does not contain any odd numbers. A distinction would therefore appear to exist between the meaning of 'infinite' and that of 'everything'. Eddy, however, relies upon its interpretation as 'everything' in her argument that there is no 'room' for evil; if God could be infinite but without necessarily being everything, then her argument would break down. The first problem, mentioned earlier, to be resolved is the issue of what might be termed the 'nature' of the Bible. Eddy relied on her extensive reading of – and genuinely highly considerable knowledge of – Scripture in arriving at her core principles, yet, as part of her core argument denies the reality of the physical universe (a far more radical position than that of Berkeley). What, exactly, she had read – and how she had read it – is a puzzle, given that her main argument would appear to deny the physical reality of printed copies of the Bible, and defines the physical visual sense with which Eddy might be assumed to have read her Bible as simply a generator of error, and not a 'sense' at all.

One solution to the problem that 'infinite' does not necessarily mean 'everything' might be to separate immaterial 'substance' from God's omnipotence, leaving God as infinitely powerful and infinitely good, but not definitionally 'everything'. Assuming that everything which occurs in the (apparent) universe is the result of the Holy Spirit – God's 'active force' – then, as God is infinitely good, all events must be part of that good, eliminating the possibility of illness and death. There is, nevertheless, still a problem here, albeit a less serious one, despite being logically quite similar to the problem of infinite sets. If God is truly omnipotent, i.e., has power without limits, then God can create 'anything', but for 'anything' to be truly *any thing*, it must include 'that which is impossible for God to create', or this category would be absent from the supposedly limitless set. This implies that either (i) God cannot create a problem beyond Her power to solve, or (ii) God can create such a conundrum; in either case God's powers are not unlimited, which appears to deny the possibility of true omnipotence.

This is, of course, the 'Paradox of the Stone': can God create a stone which is too heavy for Her/Him to move? Whether the answer is yes or no, a limitation is placed upon God's power. Despite seemingly not being able to possess 'strong omnipotence' as an attribute (though a small minority of scholars dispute this), as God has complete freedom of action within that which *is* possible, it does not necessarily contradict the principle that God can only create good events. Eddy's fundamental principles can therefore be justified, and the vast philosophical edifice she created can at present retain its foundations.

Eddy's philosophical system

In this book, I use the term 'Eddy's philosophical system' to stand for her main argument coupled with the 'healings' which she and her many followers regarded as empirical evidence. In this section, Eddy's philosophical system will be completed, although not yet in full detail. In the next chapter, however, in sequence with analysis forming the bulk of that chapter, the complete system will be promulgated.

Introduction to the philosophical system

From within the vast body of testimonies given by patients who had experienced relief from their symptoms, a subset are accompanied by corroborating medical opinions, and a further subset of these formed the evidence which Eddy interpreted as demonstrating the truth of her original axioms at the beginning of the argument, transforming them into confirmed hypotheses; confirmed, that is, in the sense of not empirically contradicted.

Since Eddy's death, this body of evidence has of course greatly increased in size. Previously, when setting forth Eddy's ideas, either axioms have been stated or deductions drawn from them. In this section, however, rather than advancing the argument with further stages of deduction or more axiomatic statements, the existing main argument will be bolstered by confirmatory evidence.

Completing the loop

In the physical sciences it is standard practice to form a hypothesis and then design an experiment in an attempt to either falsify or confirm the hypothesis. The results of the experiment therefore permit conclusions to be drawn about the original hypothesis, which 'completes the loop' of hypothesis, experiment, results, conclusions regarding the hypothesis. In metaphysics, however, it is highly unusual to follow this approach – but Eddy nevertheless does so precisely. If one considers her initial axioms and their immediate consequences as her hypothesis, then *every* attempt by a Christian Science practitioner at a 'healing' for a patient is an experiment, with the results if successful confirming, but not proving, the likelihood of Eddy's hypothesis as being correct.

Theological science

Great complexity surrounds the concept of theological science and Eddy's empirical metaphysics. Despite the fact that it is little known outside theological academia, theological science has been the subject of highly respected and very detailed texts, such as those by MacIntosh (1919), Torrance (1969) and Polkinghorne (1988). As a consequence, a detailed discussion of this aspect of is best left until later in this section, after the empirical evidence and some of the counterintuitive (and even bizarre) implications have been presented.

The next stage in presenting Eddy's system of thought relies on what she saw as empirical confirmation of her metaphysical principles, i.e. the disappearance of the apparent symptoms of illness upon convincing the individual in question that they are not ill or in pain.

As previously mentioned, one of the original features of Eddy's work is embodied in the one-word abbreviation by which she often referred to it: 'science'. To reiterate, she was not using this word in the Aristotelian sense of 'knowledge'; instead, she was echoing its use in the physical sciences, as she (and her more than 100,000 followers) interpreted the many 'cures' achieved by Christian Science practitioners as empirical proof (or, more correctly, probabilistic confirmation) of the validity of her initial assumptions and the corollaries resulting from them. The consequence of the above is that the next stage of the process of setting forth Eddy's work, and the philosophical system upon which it rests, requires the presentation of summaries of a selected subset of the many medically attested, apparently miraculous cures, the details of which are helpfully included in Chapter 18 of *Science and Health*, entitled 'Fruitage'. This will complete the promulgation of her philosophy in a form convenient for the subsequent analysis of its precise idealist nature and level, or otherwise, of originality; this analysis takes place in the next chapter.

Had it not been for the selection of patient testimonies Eddy provided in *Science and Health*, any researcher interested in patient outcomes would have to find a method of approaching the truly vast body of literature this now represents. A systematic approach, preferably with a logical rationale, would be a giant undertaking in and of itself. It might be assumed that a good basis for regarding the choice of empirical data would be to use only those outcomes which, in addition to the testimonies of the patients, are also documented by the attending medical professionals. However, a highly counterintuitive problem exists relating to what would conventionally be regarded as 'objective evidence'; but before describing it, it is helpful to present an analogous problem from the realm of homoeopathic medicine.

When a conventional medicine is tested for efficacy, the gold standard is a double-blind, randomised, controlled trial, in which the medicine is tested against a placebo, with neither the patient nor the experimenter knowing whether what is being administered is medicine or placebo. In the case of homoeopathy, however, no molecules of the active ingredient are present in the medicine, as the dilution achieved during its preparation can be more than ten to the power 30 times *beyond that which would reduce the initial presence of the active ingredient to a single molecule.* As the placebo by definition also has none of the active compound, any possible conventional trial will result in comparing either the placebo with something chemically indistinguishable from the placebo (i.e., no active molecules with no active molecules), or the homoeopathic medicine with something chemically indistinguishable from the medicine (again, no active molecules with no active molecules).

Returning to the topic of objective evidence regarding patients helped by Christian Science, a similarly peculiar situation to that described above exists in relation to what would normally be considered 'objective evidence'. Accompanying some patients' testimonies are X-ray pictures of the condition of the patient before and after treatment. If Christian Science is correct in its fundamental assumptions, then the condition for which the patient sought treatment did not exist. If an X-ray film shows evidence of the assumed illness, it must presumably be part of the grand illusion leading us into believing in the reality of illness. If this is the case, only two possibilities seem to be available: firstly, anyone looking at the X-ray film is mistaken regarding what they believe that they are seeing; and secondly, the X-ray equipment and/or film has been misled in the same manner as a sentient, human observer could be. That a supposedly non-sentient medical device could have a false belief would appear not to be a coherent claim, thus leaving the human belief regarding the X-ray picture as the source of error. The 'objective evidence', or, rather, the human beliefs regarding the 'objective evidence', therefore cannot be regarded in this manner.

Theology as an Empirical Science (MacIntosh 1919)

MacIntosh published an exceptionally detailed suggestion for what could form a future empirically scientific theology, but despite the thought and erudition which is evident throughout, its focus on the physical world makes it of less application to Eddy's work than the work of the next two authors.

Science and Creation (Polkinghorne 1988)

John Polkinghorne FRS, a professor of mathematical physics and additionally an ordained minister in the Church of England, addressed this subject in his 1988 book, *Science and Creation* (a potentially misleading choice of title, as the book has no connection with the fundamentalist doctrine expressed in the discipline known as 'Creation Science' within which the universe is sometimes asserted to be approximately 6000 years old). Given his dual qualifications to write this work, it is unsurprisingly excellent, and ideal with regard to this work.

Theological Science (Torrance 1969)

Theological science, insofar as it exists at all, 'entails an epistemological inversion[23]', by which is meant that it is normally the case in science that it is 'we who know, we observe, we examine, we inquire'[24], but in theological science it is the subject of our science, i.e. God, who knows, who observes and who examines. Eddy, however, reframes theological science as empirical metaphysics, bringing it within the methodology of the physical sciences while still denying the existence of physical reality. This is consistent with Torrance's view that: 'A

---

23. Torrance 1969, p. 131.
24. Ibid., p. 131.

primary requirement is that scientific questions must be genuine questions aimed at reality. Questions are not genuine if we already know the answer; they are only poses that do not get us anywhere but rather hold us back'[25].

Eddy's work as empirical theological science

Christian Science thus clearly sits within the frameworks outlined by MacIntosh, Polkinghorne and Torrance, and it is notable that all three of these conceptual metasystems appeared after Eddy's death. Her work cannot therefore be criticised as having been artificially forced into these schema, but instead, due to its coherence, consistency and methodology, falls naturally into them.

The philosophical system itself

It is now possible to move on to the re-expression of Eddy's system of thought. The promulgation of a restructured and partially rephrased expression of Eddy's system of thought has involved the identification of a core set of principles, initially treated as axiomatic, upon which the complex structure of her main argument could be constructed. Most importantly, from Eddy's point of view, the complete system of her Science succeeds or fails on the basis of its results; this consequently necessitated an analysis of the nature of science and what would constitute a theological science.

The next step

Setting forth Eddy's system of thought in this manner, although interesting in its own right, has been done for the purpose of analysing it with regard to the idealist philosophy, or more accurately, idealist philosophies, that it embodies. Some of Eddy's concepts appeared in the published academic philosophy of the German idealists long before the 1875 publication of *Science and Health*, and others in the writing of various British idealists who were approximately contemporaneous with her, but a small yet highly significant set of components of her idealist thought appears to be both original and

---

25. Ibid., p. 123.

still unique to Eddy, even over a century after her death. It is this analysis to which I will now turn.

In this section the internal consistency of Eddy's system of thought will be analysed, expressed in the form of ten propositions chosen from Chapter 10 of *Science and Health*[26] and rephrased for convenience. Consistency has to be distinguished from coherency, however, and even if these ten propositions are consistent with respect to each other, this does not necessarily imply that they are coherent individually; for example, it is entirely possible for two incoherent ideas to be mutually consistent. The vital and complex investigation into the coherency of Eddy's concepts therefore has a lengthy chapter of its own immediately following this one.

Although Eddy offers a core a set of 32 quasi-formal propositions in her chapter, it is too large a number to permit an exhaustive test of consistency for pairs of propositions. The number of possible pairs from n items, not taking order into account, is $n(n-1)/2$, so for 32 propositions this would be $32 \times 31 / 2 = 496$. Writing even four sentences on each combination would yield around 50,000 words, a figure which is clearly not helpful in this context. However, the ten selected propositions encompass the concepts elucidated from Eddy's system, but in a form small enough to permit every possible pair of comparisons to be made; for ten propositions, this figure is $10 \times 9 / 2 = 45$ comparisons.

Emerging from this large amount of analysis are a much smaller number of repeated themes. Some of these introduce what appear to have been completely novel concepts at the time of their publication, whereas other concepts arising from the analysis occasionally coincide with ideas expressed by the British idealists, either contemporaneously with, or, in a small number of cases, prior to, their academic publication.

The propositions selected for the purpose of this chapter (but retaining Eddy's numbering for clarity in referencing) are below, edited but not yet rephrased:

> I. God is infinite… The infinite… is unknown, and thus a knowledge of it is left either to human conjecture or to the revelation of divine Science.

---

26. Eddy 1910, pp. 330 ff.

II. God is... Life, Truth, Love. Spirit is divine Principle, and divine Principle is Love, and Love is Mind.

III. The notion that both evil and good are real is a delusion of material sense... Evil is nothing, no thing, mind, nor power.

V. Nothing possesses reality nor existence except divine Mind and His ideas.

VI. God is individual, incorporeal. ... There is no other self-existence. He is all-inclusive... He fills all space... Hence all is Spirit and spiritual.

VII. Life, Truth, and Love constitute the triune Person called God.

VIII. Father-Mother is the name for Deity.

XIV. The spiritual idea, Christ, dwells forever in the bosom of the Father, God.

XV. The invisible Christ was imperceptible Christ was imperceptible to the so-called personal senses, whereas Jesus appeared as a bodily existence.

XX. Reality is spiritual, harmonious, immutable, immortal, divine, [and] eternal.[27]

These are then reworded for simplicity and clarity as follows:

I. God is infinite and unknowable, except by divine revelation and human conjecture.

II. God is Life, Truth, Love, Spirit, Principle, Mind and Good.

III. The hypothetical construct 'evil' is a 'delusion of material sense'.

V. Nothing possesses reality or existence except divine Mind and His ideas.

VI. God fills all space, therefore all is Spirit.

VII. The triune nature of God consists of Life, Truth and Love.

VIII. God is Father-Mother.

XIV. The idea of Christ (not the human form) is eternal.

---

27. Eddy 1910, pp. 330-35.

> XV. The invisible Christ appears to the spiritual sense.
> XX. Reality is spiritual, harmonious, immutable, immortal, divine, [and] eternal.[28]

The figure of 45 comparisons arises from the fact that the first proposition can be compared with the remaining nine, the second with the remaining eight, and so forth until the penultimate proposition, which can only be compared with the last one in the sequence. The total is therefore the sum of the integers from nine descending to one, so the complete sum is simply $9 + 8 + 7 + 6 + 5 + 4 + 3 + 2 + 1 = 45$.

Testing Eddy's ideas for internal consistency

Before embarking on this task, there is a vitally important issue which must be addressed first.

One aspect of Eddy's system which only becomes apparent after considerable reading of her work is that a conflict exists between, firstly, her many assertions that matter is nothing (i.e., no thing), the belief in matter being a human error, her impressively argued conclusion that all is Spirit and Spirit occupies all space, and secondly, her seemingly contradictory statement that while Christ was an eternal, spiritual entity, Jesus was *corporeal and material*. Before attempting to provide a solution to this difficulty, it is instructive to consider examples of the above taken exclusively from the 1910 edition of *Science and Health*, this being by far her most reworked text and therefore presumably the most reconsidered.

The universe as purely spiritual

Eddy offers many examples, the following being a very small subset:

> Matter is the unreal.[29]
> Matter is a human concept.[30]
> All space is filled by God.[31]

---

28. Edited and reworded from Eddy 1910, pp. 330-35.
29. Eddy 1910, p. 468.
30. Ibid., p. 469.
31. Ibid., p. 469.

To infinite spirit there is no matter.[32]
Man is not matter; he is not made up of brain, blood, bones, and other material elements.[33]
Man is made in the image and likeness of God.[34]
Matter is not that likeness.[35]
Mortal man is [italics in the original] is really a self-contradictory phrase for man is not mortal.[36]
When he substance of Spirit appears in Christian Science, the nothingness of matter is revealed.[37]
We acknowledge the nothingness of matter.[38]

The universe as including material existence

The following single quote illustrates the potential difficulty:

> The dual personality of the unseen and the seen, the spiritual and the material, the eternal Christ and the corporeal Jesus manifest in flesh, continued until the Master's ascension, the human, *material concept* [my italics], or Jesus, disappeared, while the spiritual self, or Christ, continues to exist in the eternal order of divine Science, taking away the sins of the world, as the Christ has always done, even before the human Jesus was *incarnate to mortal eyes* [my italics].[39]

One possible resolution to this apparent conflict is provided by text Eddy wrote on the related subject of so-called (as she described it) mortal mind.

Having introduced the term on page 50 in the plural, on page 71 in the singular and then woven the thread through the subsequent

---

32. Ibid., p. 475.
33. Ibid., p. 475.
34. Ibid., p. 475.
35. Ibid., p. 475.
36. Ibid., p. 478.
37. Ibid., p. 480.
38. Ibid., p. 497.
39. Ibid., p. 334.

tapestry, it suddenly unravels at page 487 when Eddy explains that 'There is *in reality* [my italics] no such thing as *mortal* [Eddy's italics] mind.'

This may seem alarming at first: is Eddy admitting that something has been seriously in error for the many preceding pages? Thankfully, one can conclude not. The concept of mortal mind is simply a conceptual device forming a central part of the clever, subtle and sustained argument presented by her main text.

Analogies

Although imperfect, the following arguments taken from two quite diverse sources and fields of endeavour offer an approach to understanding Eddy's form of argument. The scenarios, all from a very different paradigm, relate to Aristotelian physics and compound optical microscopy.

Firstly, microscopy. An optical microscope consists of a set of small but powerful, interchangeable objective lenses which create an initial image. In explaining how the microscope functions, students can be shown that this first image can be projected on to a ground glass screen. Above the objective lenses, at the end of a short tube, the eyepiece is placed, operating exactly like a magnifying glass except acting upon the first image, rather than an object. Many students are surprised when, if the screen is removed, the microscope functions exactly as before.

In this analogy, it is the screen, not the image, which equivalent to mortal mind. Optical microscopes do not have such a screen, but the final image is still present nonetheless. Similarly, the image of Mind maintains its eternal existence even when the concept of mortal mind, introduced merely as an explanatory device, has been abandoned.

Secondly, Aristotle. It has long been the case that Aristotelian physics has been derided by those teaching the modern physics at high school level and beyond, but in a recent paper, the internationally respected physicist and author Carlo Rovelli argues persuasively that Aristotle's ideas do indeed apply to the domain under consideration[40].

---

40. Rovelli 2015.

At a key point in the paper he explains that:

> I reformulate and derive Aristotle's physics in modern terms... Therefore this is not a paper in [the] history of science; I do not look at Aristotle from his own time's perspective, but rather from the perspective of a later time. ... Here I compare the two theories of physics which have had the largest and longest success in the history of humanity, as a contemporary scientist would describe them: in technical terms.[41]

Rovelli then summarises Aristotle's understanding of motion as follows:

> Natural motion... is of two different kinds, according to whether it is motion of the Ether or motion of one of the four [classical] elements Earth, Water, Air and Fire.
> 1. The natural motion of the Ether in Heaven is circular and around the center;
> 2. The natural motion of Earth, Water, Air and Fire is vertical, directed towards *the natural place of the substance*. [my italics][42]

That last phrase refers to Aristotle's idea that different substances (as we would describe them) have differing densities, stratifying them in a 'fluid' medium (a term which in physics includes air).

Rovelli then re-expresses the above algebraically and demonstrates that *on earth, in air*, Aristotle's description of motion was correct. Amusingly, he points out that Aristotle did *not* say that heavier objects fall faster than light objects if you take away all the air! Given that Aristotle did not think a vacuum could exist, this scenario was not even considered by him.

The analogy in this case is not the content, but the fact that when interpreted correctly, in the precisely defined domain to which it applies, systems of thought which have been dismissed as simply wrong reveal themselves to have been correct all along. The domain

---

41. Rovelli 2015, p. 23.
42. Ibid., p. 24.

in the case of the fragment of Christian Science in question is not Christian Science itself or its philosophical underpinning, but *Eddy's argument*.

All of the above is vital to the next step, in which the argument relating to materiality is completed, hopefully resolving what would otherwise be a fundamental inconsistency and incoherency in Eddy's ideas. I suggest that just as *illusory* mortal mind was merely a helpful explanatory device, Eddy's references to corporeality are mileposts on the way to her final destination. The nonexistence of material substance and therefore corporeality can be explicitly seen in many quotes from *Science and Health*, and crucially, Eddy states that *the corporeal Jesus appeared to material senses*, which throughout all her work she stresses as in reality not senses, but generators of illusion. A particularly helpful passage appears on page 477:

> To the five corporeal senses, man appears to be matter and mind united; but Christian Science reveals man as the idea of God, and declares the corporeal senses to be mortal illusions.[43]

Bearing all of the above in mind, we can now approach the analysis of the chosen propositions summarising Eddy's system of thought.

Comparisons involving Proposition I: God is infinite and unknowable, except by divine revelation and human conjecture

I and II God is Life, Truth, Love, Spirit, Principle, Mind and Soul

God as unknowable except by these modes is unaffected by Eddy's 'scientific definition of God' using what she termed the 'seven synonyms'). For these terms to be applicable they must have been revealed by God or be Eddy's conjecture.

---

43. Eddy 1910, p. 477.

I and III The hypothetical construct 'evil' is a 'delusion of material sense'

The nonexistence of evil requires both divine revelation, as a starting point, and human reasoning from there onwards. That God is good is either divine revelation or part of the definition of God (or both); that therefore evil cannot exist is a human deduction.

I and V Nothing possesses reality or existence except divine Mind and His ideas

The specified modes of acquiring knowledge of God may not be the only approach with regard to (at least) some ideas of the divine Mind. I assume that these can be perceived by the spiritual sense, as only God and His/Her divine ideas are truly real.

I and VI God fills all space, therefore all is Spirit

Eddy's understanding of the word 'infinite' is that it is synonymous with the word 'unlimited'. Consequently, given that this is a known truth regarding God's attributes, it must be either divine revelation, or human conjecture, or both. An intermediate possibility is that it could be the result of divinely guided human conjecture.

I and VII The triune nature of God consists of Life, Truth and Love

Eddy's understanding of the Trinity must have been acquired by either divine revelation or human conjecture. As Eddy has stated throughout her many works, Christian Science is a form of revealed truth (although the exact wording changed at times during the 432 editions of *Science and Health*); it would be instructive to map the extent of this aspect in Eddy's work as opposed to subsequent deductions made from this revealed truth.

I and VIII God is Father-Mother

This could be seen as a novel consequence of God's infinite nature. If 'infinite' is interpreted as 'unlimited', then it cannot be the case that God is limited to only one gender, or, indeed, only two; God as having an infinite number of genders would appear to be the only possible conclusion.

I and XIV *The idea of Christ (not the human form) is eternal*

Although God is only knowable by divine revelation or (valid) human conjecture, Christ's attributes are more readily apparent, as his literal 'appearance' in human form is in part due to his role as the only mediator between God and mankind.

I and XV *The invisible Christ appears to the spiritual sense*

Although the invisible Christ appears only to the spiritual sense, the conditions regarding gaining knowledge of God do not include the application of this sensory mode, adding to the distinction between God and Christ.

I and XX *Reality is spiritual, harmonious, immutable, immortal, divine, [and] eternal*

Although what we know of God is by revelation and conjecture, 'definitional' properties are also relevant, and all of the above are consistent with attributes of God.

Comparisons involving Proposition II God is Life, Truth, Love, Spirit, Principle, Mind and Soul

II and III *The hypothetical construct 'evil' is a 'delusion of material sense'*

Although not a complete description of God (as none ever can be), the seven so-called 'synonyms' of Eddy's 'scientific' definition of God do serve to highlight the idea that evil, and all that is associated with it, is the error of man's imagination, and no part either of God or of God's works.

II and V *Nothing possesses reality or existence except divine Mind and His ideas*

Combining Eddy's so-called scientific definition of God with the concept that nothing is real except God and His/Her divine ideas leads to the corollary that only Life, Truth, Love, Spirit, Principle, Mind and Good can exist, along with God's ideas.

II and VI God fills all space, therefore all is Spirit

The combination of Propositions II and VI imply that all space is completely filled with all that exists, namely, that which is described by the seven synonyms Eddy used to characterise God: Life, Love, Truth, Spirit, Principle, Mind and Good. Each of these terms, despite Eddy's claim of 'synonymity', deserves separate analysis.

II and VII The triune nature of God consists of Life, Truth and Love

Curiously, Eddy uses three of the seven synonyms of the 'scientific definition of God' to represent the three elements (normally referred to as 'persons' in conventional theology) of the Trinity. In Christian Science, however, the word 'Trinity' is defined and used differently, describing differing characteristics of a non-triune God (at least in the conventional sense of the word).

II and VIII God is Father-Mother

It follows from these two premises that God as Father-Mother must be representable by the 'scientific definition of God', implying that the Mother aspect of God's characteristics shares these descriptions. A non-physical reality potentially leaves the stereotypical roles associated with gender untouched, while conceivably eliminating sexual differences, assuming that they are purely physical and have an analogue in Eddy's spiritual reality. This could result in the gender roles being societal constructs and the assumed sexual dimorphism being neither a societal construction nor a biological one, but merely an error in keeping with error of belief in pain, illness and death.

II and XIV The idea of Christ (not the human form) is eternal

This a potentially weak point in Christian Science, covered in the earlier discussion regarding materiality.

II and XV The invisible Christ appears to the spiritual sense

Whereas Proposition II is a definition, Proposition XV is an assertion following from a definition. The invisible Christ perceived through spiritual sense is one example of this (only true) mode of perception.

II and XX Reality is spiritual, harmonious, immutable, immortal, divine [and] eternal

This comparison can be thought of as simply an exposition of the attributes of God, who by any definition will be harmonious to Herself/Himself.

Comparisons involving Proposition III The hypothetical construct 'evil' is a 'delusion of material sense'

III and V Nothing possesses reality or existence except divine Mind and His ideas

A further argument Eddy uses to deduce the nonexistence of evil relies on her assertion that God occupies space – namely, all space. If, as Eddy so defines it within Christian Science, evil is analogously defined as also needing to occupy space, then clearly the only possible conclusion is that evil cannot exist. Both of these spatial concepts are consistent with Eddy's statements on this issue throughout her many other works besides *Science and Health*.

III and VI God fills all space, therefore all is Spirit

Proposition III taken in conjunction with Proposition V fits into the pattern of Eddy's repeated assertion (albeit in different forms) that as God is good and God, by virtue of being unlimited, is everything, then everything must be good. Evil, sickness and death, within the system of thought represented by Christian Science, therefore cannot exist, and are the result of erroneous human conjecture.

III and VII The triune nature of God consists of Life, Truth and Love

The triune nature of God, reflecting the attributes of God, clearly cannot and does not reflect the nonexistent construct, 'evil'.

III and VIII God is Father-Mother

These two statements, Proposition III and Proposition VIII, although they do not support each other, neither do they contradict each other's assertions. They are therefore in that very limited sense supportive.

III and XIV The idea of Christ (not the human form) is eternal

Proposition III and Proposition XIV, while not addressing non-overlapping magisteria, nevertheless appear to have no overlap of meaning. Therefore, although they are clearly not inconsistent as a result, neither are they literally supportive of each other.

III and XV The invisible Christ appears to the spiritual sense

Proposition III and Proposition XV make a very interesting pair, as they raise different sides of one specific issue. Central to Christian Science is the concept of spiritual sense; what we normally think of as the physical senses are, in Christian Science, merely creators of error. The invisible Christ appears solely to the spiritual sense, whereas the delusion of evil appears only to the physical (non-) senses.

III and XX Reality is spiritual, harmonious, immutable, immortal, divine [and] eternal

This is consistent with evil, pain, illness and death not being part of reality.

Comparisons involving Proposition V Nothing possesses reality or existence except divine Mind and His ideas

V and VI God fills all space, therefore all is Spirit

Proposition V very clearly follows from Proposition VI, which uses the word 'all' twice in its assertion that all is God, and as God is Spirit, all is Spirit. Having made this statement, the divine Mind is consequently part of the 'all', as are ideas generated by the divine Mind. Despite Eddy's assertion of a spiritual reality, Christian Science makes the highly unusual claim that spiritual entities, including God, occupy space. This assertion is unique within the metaphysical family of religions, and also within the variety of forms loosely grouped together under the generic term 'American transcendentalism'.

V and VII The triune nature of God consists of Life, Truth and Love

Nothing possesses reality except the divine Mind and His/Her ideas. Therefore, as Proposition VII relates to the 'inner' God, it is consistent.

V and VIII God is Father-Mother

In conventional Trinitarian Christian theology, God is Father, Son and Holy Ghost. In Christian Science, however, Eddy redefines God as Father/Mother. Christ within Christian Science must be a divine idea of God, but nevertheless appears to exist within a hierarchy of concepts.

V and XIV The idea of Christ (not the human form) is eternal

In Eddy's system, Christ is subordinate to God, being a divine idea of God, rather than a 'person' of the triune God himself. Additionally, Christ is the unique role of being the mediator between God and mankind, further emphasising the separation between God and mankind within Christian Science; this is just one example of the many tenets which were viewed as blasphemous by contemporary theologians (as some twenty-first-century theologians still do). As the divine idea of God, Christ must be subordinate to God, yet eternal and changeless, as if divine thoughts changed with time, this would presumably imply some change in God, which is excluded within the definition. Oddly, this concept seems immediately capable of generalisation. If all that exists is God and His/Her divine ideas, and if divine ideas are changeless in the above manner, then (spiritual) reality should be changeless, intriguingly echoing the conclusion of Parmenides (discussed elsewhere), despite being the conclusion of a completely different style of argument.

V and XV The invisible Christ appears to the spiritual sense

This is consistent with all true reality being Spirit. Soul must therefore also be Spirit and eternal. Christ can therefore in turn be seen as an eternal soul with the unique additional property of being the sole mediator between God and mankind.

V and XX Reality is spiritual, harmonious, immutable, immortal, divine [and] eternal

Proposition V addresses what might be termed the 'structure' of spiritual reality, whereas Proposition XX is concerned with its content; they are therefore harmonious.

Comparisons involving Proposition VI God fills all space, therefore all is Spirit

VI and VII The triune nature of God consists of Life, Truth and Love

God is defined as filling 'all space' in Christian Science is an interesting variation on the concept of 'infinitely large', analogous to a more conventional definition of infinity as strong omnipotence is in relation to its more typical interpretation. It is possible for something to be infinitely large without it filling 'all space'.

VI and VIII God is Father-Mother

This is a particularly interesting combination. Proposition VI, taken in conjunction with Proposition VIII presumably mean that all space, and therefore the entire universe and everything within it, is ungendered., and beyond this, sexually non-dimorphic. It is difficult to image a more prescient statement. The issue of gender identity is widely discussed on at present, but the denial of sexual difference is largely unknown outside academia, and even here it is a minority view. Butler's work[44] is an example of this rarely voiced strand of thought. In *Gender Trouble: Feminism and the Subversion of Identity* Butler considers the works of Sigmund Freud, Simone de Beauvoir, Julia Kristeva, Jacques Lacan, Luce Irigaray, Monique Wittig, Jacques Derrida and Michel Foucault, Butler's argument being that the categories of sex, gender and sexuality are cultural constructs resulting from repeated stylised actions. Although these acts create the appearance of an ontological gender, Butler asserts that gender, sex and sexuality are performative, explicitly challenging biological accounts of binary sexual categories. Instead, Butler argues that 'disciplinary regimes' predetermine the set

---

44. Butler 1990, pp. xxviii-xxix.

of possibilities of gender, sexuality and crucially, of sex, which are given permission to appear as 'natural'. The supposedly intrinsic nature of sex as a natural category demonstrates to how deeply its production in discourse is concealed. 'Sexes', once imposed as a physical 'fact', is the framework for constructions of gender and sexuality. Butler believes that one should not seek to define 'women', arguing instead for the idea of identity as free. Although a daring intellectual position, it is arguably less so than Eddy's denial of the entirety of physical reality.

VI and XIV The idea of Christ (not the human form) is eternal

This pair of concepts create the possibility of speculation, rather than analysis, as they are not obviously linked. As all is Spirit, and the Spiritual Christ is eternal, the former statement refers to space, whereas the latter does with regard to time.

VI and XV The invisible Christ appears to the spiritual sense

Christ's status as a spirit is consistent with all real existence being spiritual, but Christ as the only mediator between God and mankind is by definition a unique status, and as such needs further analysis.

VI and XX Reality is spiritual, harmonious, immutable, immortal, divine [and] eternal

As in an earlier comparison, this refers to 'structure' and 'content', and is harmonious, as before.

Comparisons involving Proposition VII The triune nature of God consists of Life, Truth and Love

VII and VIII God is Father-Mother

Eddy completely redefines the term 'Trinity', used in conventional, mainstream Christianity to stand for 'The Father, the Son and the Holy Spirit', in terms used elsewhere in Christian Science. Although Proposition VII is not inconsistent with Proposition VIII, this is because the two propositions address very different aspects of the underlying philosophy.

VII and XIV The idea of Christ (not the human form) is eternal

These two propositions, Proposition VII and Proposition XIV, although both from within the same academic subject, nevertheless address non-overlapping magisteria. Eddy's highly controversial definition of God as Father/Mother (still controversial now, in the twenty-first century, let alone in the nineteenth) can deflect serious analysis from the issue actually under discussion.

VII and XV The invisible Christ appears to the spiritual sense

Expanding on Eddy's assertion that all is Spirit, that Spirit occupies space and that God, as unlimited (but composed of Spirit) must occupy all space, the divine ideas, presumably cannot occupy space, as Eddy is quite explicit that there is none left! This creates the apparent contradiction that

1. Divine ideas exist.
2. All that exists is Spirit.
3. God's Spirit occupies all space.

Either divine ideas are part of the Spirit forming all reality, or they do not appear to be able to exist.

VII and XX Reality is spiritual, harmonious, immutable, immortal, divine [and] eternal

Eddy's redefinition of the Trinity is entirely consistent with Proposition XX.

Comparisons involving Proposition VIII God is Father-Mother

VIII and XIV The idea of Christ (not the human form) is eternal

That God as Father-Mother is eternal is entirely consistent with the eternality of the Spiritual Christ. In the case of the Trinity as conventionally defined, all three 'persons' clearly must be co-eternal.

VIII and XV The invisible Christ appears to the spiritual sense

Eddy's radical statement that God is Father-Mother has the corollary that, if (as is not the case in earlier proposition combinations in this sequence) one assumes that Christ is not similarly bigendered, then this adds an extra layer of reasoning behind Eddy's exclusion of Christ from her definition of the Trinity.

VIII and XX Reality is spiritual, harmonious, immutable, immortal, divine [and] eternal

Eddy's concept of God as Father-Mother has a symmetry to it which is arguably more harmonious than mainstream versions, and is therefore consistent.

Comparison involving Proposition XIV The idea of Christ (not the human form) is eternal

XIV and XV The invisible Christ appears to the spiritual sense

The idea of Christ is spiritual and therefore real. The 'image', i.e. the 'physical form' cannot be real; non-Spirit is unreal and the non-eternal also lacks reality. The physical 'senses', even if they were as such, cannot perceive spiritual reality, and are therefore merely sources of error.

XIV and XX Reality is spiritual, harmonious, immutable, immortal, divine [and] eternal

Christ, in eternal form, is clearly harmonious, and thus the comparison is consistent.

Comparisons involving Proposition XV The invisible Christ appears to the spiritual sense

XV and XX Reality is spiritual, harmonious, immutable, immortal, divine [and] eternal

As all reality is spiritual, this is self-evidently consistent.

Moving on

Having considered the internal consistency of Eddy's system, it is now necessary to examine her ideas in full philosophical depth, analysing them to see if the concepts they express are coherent in themselves.

Chapter 8

Eddy's Radicalism

Problems and Solutions

Several themes have resulted from the analysis in the previous chapters. They include strikingly original contributions made by Eddy to the philosophy of religion, facets of her belief system characterisable as the limiting case of idealism, and the entire methodology of 'empirical metaphysics', but also a number of ambiguities and potentially paradoxical statements. I suspect it is at least partly the nebulosity of Eddy's prose style, coupled with occasional near (but never actual) incoherency, which is largely responsible for the curious dearth of academic analyses of her work since her death in 1910, at least until very recently. Foremost amongst the original aspects of Eddy's philosophical system is the concept of 'empirical metaphysics', in which she copies the sequence 'hypothesis, experiment, results, conclusion' from the physical sciences. This relies on her idea that, although matter does not exist, space does, and in her system of thought, spirit, although a non-physical substance, nevertheless requires space in which to exist. It is this latter concept which permits the major deductions Eddy makes from her initial axioms, such as the nonexistence of evil and illness, for example.

A major source of ambiguity is the somewhat variable degree to which Eddy considered that spiritual sense differs from what we (wrongly, according to Eddy) imagine to be our physical sense. For example, in the case of the Bible, for this to serve as Eddy's 'initial data' then the spiritual sense by which she claims that it is perceived must have a perfect correlation with our original conception. With a (supposedly) ill patient, however, the 'physical sense' and spiritual sense differ with regard to the existence of the patient's illness. Any situation in which the physical 'senses' suggest that only evil is present must imply that the correct, spiritual-sense perception of the same situation is completely different.

The most curious aspects of Christian Science are where Mary Baker Eddy seems almost overly specific. Whereas her arguments about the nature of existence begin with simply stated premises, some of her definitions are, to say the least, puzzling. A good example of this tendency is her 'scientific' definition of God, in which she uses the seven 'synonyms'. This is odd in at least three different ways: firstly, unlike her arguably correct use of the word 'science' (in the modern sense) when applied to Christian Science as a whole, the definition she offers for God does not appear to be scientific at all; secondly, the seven terms used are not synonyms; and thirdly, how was this set determined? If it was divine revelation then my criticisms are of course wrong, but if it is human conjecture (though some claimed, and others still claim, that Mary Baker Eddy was, and even still is, very much more than human, as previously described) the possibility of error remains.

Potential problems

One of the problematic areas of Mary Baker Eddy's system, as was briefly alluded to earlier, is her used of the word 'infinite' to mean 'unlimited', and thereby 'everything'. The logical difficulty which this presents may not be obvious if the reader is unfamiliar with either higher mathematics or symbolic logic, but is extremely well known within these fields. Russell's Paradox[1], as it is often known, is as follows: consider the set of all sets which are not members of themselves – is it a member of itself? If one answers 'yes', then the fact of its inclusion means that, by the definition above it must be removed from the 'superset', but having done so, now that it is no longer a member of itself, it should be reincluded, recreating the earlier situation which caused its removal. The question therefore *cannot be answered either 'yes' or 'no'*. The point of this paradox is to highlight the curious problems which surround the concept of 'everything'. If we create a set which we believe to include 'everything', then if it does not include itself, it cannot logically be everything. If we then add the

---

1. Russell 1903, p. 101.

set itself as a member of itself, we have changed the contents of the original set (i.e. it now contains itself as an element, and is therefore no longer the original set in question), and so this new set must be included as an element. This clearly leads to an infinite series of extra inclusions, with a set that really is 'everything' always out of reach.

An extension of the argument which leads to the same conclusion is as follows: any set, whether finite or infinite, has a series of subsets which can be formed from it. For example, the set {a,b,c} generates the subsets {a}, {b}, {c}, {a, b}, {a, c} and {b, c}. In pure mathematics, the empty set {} and the complete set {a, b, c} are also considered as being subsets, making eight in all. This figure is 2 to the power of the number of elements, so it increases rapidly with the size of the set; a set with just 20 elements has 1,048,576 subsets. Returning to the case of an infinite set, it has 2 to the power infinity subsets, which, if the original set is to be genuinely everything, must be included, as the subsets are of course 'things'. With the new set, with vastly more elements, we now face the same problem, i.e. that we need to include all of its subsets, which naturally creates a third set, with again very many more elements. Every time we include the subsets, we create a new, larger set, which then has to have its subsets included, and so in an infinite series of extra inclusions, never attaining 'everything' within a set. Applying the above to Mary Baker Eddy's concept of God as 'everything' could be considered as demonstrating an element of incoherency of this definition. Alternatively, however, it can be viewed as a window through which we see both a new field of mathematics, its surprising importance to mainstream theology and its particular centrality to Christian Science.

The mathematics in question is that discovered by Georg Cantor at the end of the nineteenth century. Cantor set forth the theory of transfinite numbers, all of which are infinite, but all are also in fixed positions in a hierarchy of infinities; this is described in great detail in Ferreirós (2007). The lowest transfinite number, termed Aleph null or Aleph zero, describes the total number of integers. Aleph 1, in turn, denotes the total number of 'real' numbers, i.e. those involving recurring or non-recurring decimals. A breathtakingly elegant proof due to Cantor, known as the Diagonal Argument[2] demonstrates the fact that this number is greater than the number of integers. Beyond these, an infinity of transfinite numbers extends upwards, but there is

---

2. Cantor 1895.

a set-theoretical concept, Absolute Infinity, denoted using the Greek capital letter Omega, which is beyond all of them. Fascinatingly, it has so far defied mathematicians' attempts to precisely define it[3]. Polkinghorne has suggested that this may form what could be termed apophatic mathematics[4].

The term 'apophatic theology' in writing about God has been a part of Christian theology since the early-sixth-century author Pseudo-Dionysius. However, the use of negation in relation to God has a longer history than Christianity, reaching back to the Hebrew scriptures and even before the era of classical Greek philosophy. Although theologians and others have always affirmed something of God, either as a result of speculation about the Divine or as an communication of revelation about God, these statements have always retained the mysteriousness of the Divine, leading to the negating of any emphatic statements about God, thus acknowledging the inadequacy of any human conceptions about God.

However, Rucker (the great-great-great grandson of G.W.F. Hegel) reverses the analogy, suggesting instead that 'set theory could form a precise theology'[5]. It is the existence of Omega as a rigorous yet undefined mathematical concept which gives a possible solution to Eddy's otherwise problematic use of the word 'infinite'.

Potential strengths

One of the very strong themes which emerge from the analytical comparisons are issues relating to the conception of Christ and God within Christian Science. Beginning with her strikingly courageous assertion that God is Father-Mother, we find her complete redefinition of the Trinity. Christ now has precisely two roles in Eddy's system: communicating to mankind a set of vital truths and acting as the sole mediator between God and mankind. The aforementioned truths are also radical. Firstly, Christ sought to explain that the Kingdom of God is already here (rather than appearing during the 'end times' of future history). Secondly, and perhaps even more surprisingly, the 'correct' interpretation of Matthew v. 48 ('Be ye therefore perfect, even as your Father which is in heaven is perfect') is that God, as a perfect being,

---

3. Polkinghorne 1988, p. 81.
4. Ibid., p. 81.
5. Rucker 1982, p. 81.

would not create an imperfect being; mankind is therefore already perfect; it is not a command to seek to attain perfection, but the pronouncement of the truth that mankind is already perfect. Thirdly, and most originally of all, is the mechanism by which Christ 'healed' the sick: he succeeded in explaining to them that sickness is unreal.

Next in importance are pairings involving Eddy's concept that 'only that which is eternal is real'. Assuming mankind to be real, mankind must be eternal; this is consistent with man being the divine idea of God, and the concept of God being changeless; if God's divine ideas are changeless, and if mankind is one of these ideas, mankind must be changeless and therefore eternal.

As discussed earlier, Mary Baker Eddy's reliance on Scripture is only coherent if the Bible can be perceived through spiritual sense, as those which are normally thought of as the physical senses are in reality simply a source of erroneous thoughts, not sense impressions. As we have just seen, for something to be truly real, it must be eternal, and assuming that Eddy considered the Bible to be real (a fair bet) then the Bible must be eternal. This is strongly suggestive of the Christ-Jesus duality, in that as an invisible form, Christ has existed eternally, but as a visible form (Jesus) only for a finite time. This idea can be applied to Scripture, i.e. that Scripture has always existed invisibly as the word of God, but the visible form only began to be written around 3500 years ago. The Bible considered as the revealed Truth of God is in its written form the result of having been – to an extent at least – 'dictated' to the writer of each book.

This is of course also how Eddy viewed her main work, *Science and Health* (1910), and the above visible/invisible duality may be applied in this case. As the revealed ideas of God, the ideas themselves must have existed eternally, whereas the written, visible form, only since the date of publication. However, assuming this to be the case, perhaps Eddy was plagiarising God, and therefore should not have sought to own the copyright.

The duality concept can be extended much further, having an intriguing similarity with Plato. If everything is either God or the divine ideas of God, then as God is a changeless, eternal being, these ideas must have existed eternally. All possible entities must already be in the Mind of God, representing the invisible forms, and in a subset of cases they ultimately become visible forms. But as the visible forms are only transitory, they are not fully real; only the invisible, eternal forms are truly real. It is these which I equate with Plato's ideal forms.

To infinity and beyond

Eddy's argument that God is infinite and therefore everything, hides another of her remarkably original concepts. The precise form of the argument she uses proves that as God occupies all space, all must be God; this implies that metaphysical, spiritual entities require space in which to exist. At first sight this may appear to be simply an unwise attempt to straddle the physical and the metaphysical, but in reality it is entirely consistent with her use of the word 'science' with regard to Christian Science, i.e. to close the loop of hypothesis (her axioms), experiment (attempting healings), result (the effect, or lack thereof, on the patient) and conclusion (if the patient 'recovers' then it supports the original hypothesis). It is this 'empirical metaphysics' or 'theological science' which is consistent with metaphysical entities occupying space. If sin, sickness and death are unreal, and if we assume that this unreality consists of the erroneous thoughts of mankind, then belief in these concepts must have begun at some finite time ago for them to be non-eternal. However, if the visible/invisible duality applies here, does this mean that as part of the infinite array of possible thoughts which God has already had, these ideas had already been present invisibly throughout eternity? This relates to the concept of strong omnipotence: can God have wrong ideas? If not, then surely this is a limitation, which is not congruent with Eddy's understanding of a unlimited God. Furthermore, if all that exists is God, or the divine ideas of God, how does mankind firstly make any errors at all, and secondly, upon realising their nature as error, experience a change of mind? Surely, as either a consciousness within God, or a facet of divine ideas, the possession of an erroneous idea would be impossible; furthermore, any change would imply a change in a supposedly changeless God. This, I argue, is potentially by far the most serious flaw in Eddy's system, even to the point of being catastrophic to its coherency.

Luckily, Mary Baker Eddy herself addressed this question in response to a reader's enquiry, but the truth of this will demand a very detailed explanation.

> That God is Truth, the Scriptures aver; that Truth never created error, *or such a capacity* [my italics], is self-evident… therefore your answer is that error is an illusion of mortals; that God is not its author, and it cannot be real.[6]

At first it may appear that Eddy has failed to address the question, which relates not to the initial error of a person believing themselves to be ill, but to *the capacity to make an error of this nature*, and as a consequence, has also not answered the question. However, despite the partial truth of this accusation, my reading of the above is that Eddy has hit upon something quite subtle. Before explaining why this is the case, a digression is needed into, firstly, Presocratic philosophy, and secondly, symbolic logic.

Parmenides attained genuine sophistication in the arguments he put forward for his highly counterintuitive conclusions. Unlike the slightly earlier Milesian philosophers Thales, Anaximander and Anaximenes, Parmenides was less concerned with the natural philosophy upon which these earlier figures had largely been focussed; for example 'the exiguous surviving evidence of Parmenides' astronomical system is so brief and so obscure that it is impossible with any confidence to reconstruct a coherent account of his extraordinary theory of "garlands"'[7]. Instead, his interests were often epistemological and ontological, with his conclusions resulting from following the path in which he was propelled by pure logic, as his 'metaphysics and epistemology leave no room for cosmologies such as his Ionian predecessors had constructed nor indeed for any belief at all in the world our senses disclose to us'[8].

Beginning with the premise that a vacuum cannot 'be a thing' on the basis that 'what makes something real is… that it has some predicate true of it'[9], space itself, in the sense of a vacuum, therefore fails this test, as it cannot have attributes, being nothing (i.e. no thing); it therefore follows that for Parmenides there are no gaps in the physical universe.

---

6. Eddy 1897, pp. 49-50.
7. Kirk, Raven and Schofield 1983, p. 259.
8. Ibid., p. 241.
9. Ibid., p. 246.

The importance of this seemingly prosaic fact is very great indeed, as if an object – any object – is to move, the physical location of the place into which it is to move must first be vacated of the object currently present. This, in turn, necessitates that the next space must be emptied for this new object to move. This process therefore occurs as an infinite sequence, which must be completed in order for the first object to move. As the 'last' object in any sequence has nowhere into which it can move, it follows that the entire sequence of movements cannot take place, and therefore the first object cannot move. Parmenides used this argument not merely as entertainment or as simply interesting in and of itself (which of course it is), but as proof that our 'senses' mislead us; movement appears to take place, yet it cannot.

Although arguing from entirely different first principles, Eddy can be seen as having come to the same conclusions regarding the true nature of our physical senses, which, in her words, are merely 'generators of error' and of 'false beliefs'. Other Presocratic philosophers also offered arguments supporting the idea that our senses are misleading. Zeno was the originator of a number of famous paradoxes, which although again interesting in and of themselves, are designed for a very specific purpose, namely, to suggest that at the very least we should treat our sense-data with caution. For the purpose of this book, however, one of his paradoxes is presented as an example of the curious properties of an infinite series; this forms another element in the necessary digression.

One of Zeno's paradoxes concerns Achilles and a tortoise. Achilles was famed for his running speed, and so in the story of a race with a tortoise he gives the animal a generous head start. One might assume that despite this, Achilles will swiftly overtake the creature, but Zeno presents an ingenious argument that this cannot actually take place. He explains that when Achilles catches up with the starting position of the tortoise, it will have moved forward. No matter how little the amount, the point is that the tortoise will still be ahead in what we will call Position 2. The paradox becomes apparent when, a little later, Achilles reaches Position 2; the tortoise, of course, has moved a little further still, in other words, to Position 3. It is now possible to see the problem Achilles faces in Zeno's paradox: every time he catches up with the tortoise at a given position, it has advanced a little further; it appears from the argument that he can never catch up with the tortoise, let alone overtake it. This is completely at odds with our senses, which seem to communicate the visual impression of Achilles rapidly overtaking his competitor and winning the race. Zeno therefore argues that our senses must be in some way mistaken.

In the case of Zeno's paradox of Achilles and the Tortoise, the concept at its centre which is responsible for the highly surprising apparent consequence is one from modern (Newton onwards, so approximately the period since the 1660s) pure mathematics, known as the 'limit of a series as the number of elements tends to infinity'. As an example of the idea, consider the sequence 1, 0.5, 0.25, 0.125, 0.0625… onwards, without end. The terms halve each time, ever-nearing, but never actually reaching, zero, as half of any non-zero number cannot ever be zero. What Zeno didn't appreciate, however (and in fairness to him, neither did anyone else for about 2000 years after his creation of the paradox), is that even though all of the terms of the sequence are non-zero, and despite the series' infinite number of terms, its sum – that is its sum to infinity, adding together an infinite number of terms – is both *finite and calculable*.

In the case of this abstract example, one can determine the total using the following formula:

Sum to infinity $= a / (1 - r)$

This surprisingly simple formula – surprising in relation to the complexity of an infinite number of additions – can be proved using Newton's discovery of integral calculus, but even without this modest level of sophistication, there is still a very elegant proof available:

sum to infinity $= a + ar + ar^2 + ar^3 + \ldots$
therefore: $r \times$ sum to infinity $= ar + ar^2 + ar^3 + \ldots$
therefore: $r \times$ sum to infinity $=$ sum to infinity $- a$
therefore: $r \times$ sum to infinity $-$ sum to infinity $= -a$
therefore: sum to infinity $\times (r - 1) = -a$
therefore: sum to infinity $= -a/(r - 1) = a/(1 - r)$

In the case of this abstract example, one can therefore determine the total by putting in the values $a = 1$ and $r = 0.5$: Sum to infinity $= (1) / [1 - (0.5)] = 1/0.5 = 2$. In the above, '$a$' is the first term (in this case 1) and 'r' is the common ratio between each successive pair of terms (in this case 0.5). The connection with Zeno's paradox is that, in each analysis of the tortoise's successive new positions, it has moved forwards by an ever-smaller amount corresponding to the common ratio 'r' in the formula, with the first term, 'a', being the first amount that the tortoise moves before Achilles catches up with the tortoise's first position.

The formula then provides the position at which Achilles does overtake the tortoise and explains why the paradox appears to imply that Achilles never does so. The reason is that ever-smaller 'chunks' of time are being considered, with each one being related to the immediately previous one by the ratio 'r'. In the paradox, 'r' is the tortoise's speed divided by that of Achilles; if, for example, it is 100 times slower, then $r = 0.01$. As the distance travelled during each chunk of time is directly proportional to the duration, each successive distance is also smaller. The distances therefore form a geometric series, with the sum to infinity, as before, being both finite and calculable. Zeno – and everyone else for two millennia – naturally, but wrongly, assumed that that an infinite sum of finite amounts (albeit increasingly small, finite amounts) must total infinity, meaning Achilles never overtakes the tortoise.

It is now possible to return to the earlier assertion that there is a link here with Eddy's answer to the question regarding how a person, as the perfect creation of God, can be sufficiently imperfect to make the 'errors' of belief in pain, sickness and death. Before explaining the solution, another concept from pure mathematics is needed first. As before, it involves an infinitely long sequence, but in this case the even stranger concept of a series not having a finite limit, or an infinite one – the series has no limit in the completely different sense that it doesn't exist.

An abstract example may help illustrate the concept. Imagine a sequence as below: 1, −1, 1, −1, 1, −1, 1. ... What is the 'last' term of the series if continued to infinity: one or minus one? This may seem a very long way from the original question, but we are nearly there. If there are an even number of terms, then the last term is '-1', but if there are an odd number, then the last term is '1'. What, then, is the infinite sum of this series? This explains the purpose of the previous question. If it is 1, then the series adds to one, but if it is -1, then the series adds to zero instead, because all the plus ones and minus ones cancel out. The infinite sum, therefore, relies as before on whether the number of terms in an infinite series is odd or even. Again, as before, this question does not have an answer, and therefore *the sum of the infinite series also lacks an answer.*

Finally, returning to the original question, the situation can be represented as below:

First term: making the error of belief re illness etc.;
Second term: making the error that it is possible to make the error inherent in the first term;
Third term: making the error involved in making the error in the second term;
... and so forth.

This is analogous to a sequence of Boolean 'NOT' functions from elementary symbolic logic: NOT(NOT(NOT(A))) If this sequence is continued to infinity, with an infinite incidence of 'NOT' functions, does it evaluate as A or NOT(A)? If it is an even number of NOTs, they cancel out, but if there are an odd number, they do not. Just as before, *the answer does not exist*. The original question therefore generates what in logic is known as a 'formally undecidable proposition'. Although this argument, if valid, denies the possibility that Eddy is correct, it also implies that she is *definitely not wrong*. Many far better-known historical examples of individuals known as philosophers have left major works which although greatly respected in their time are now viewed as arguing for conclusions which are simply wrong. Eddy therefore exceeds this benchmark with her system of thought.

Melissus' ideas

The similarities between Melissus' philosophy and Mary Baker Eddy's Christian Science are made strikingly apparent by the text below, taken from Burnet[10]:

1. If nothing is, what can be said of it as something real? 1a. What was ever, ever shall be. For if it had come into being it must have been nothing before it came into being. Now, if it were nothing, in no [way] could anything have arisen out of nothing.
2. Since, then, it has not come into being, and since it is, was ever, and ever shall be, it has no beginning or end, but

---

10. Burnet 1920, pp. 321 ff.

is without limit. [i.e. if it ended it would be nothing, which is impossible]

...

5. If it were not one, it would be bounded by something else.
6. For if it is [infinite] , it must be one; for if it were two, it could not be infinite; for then they would be bounded [limited] by one another.
7. So then it is eternal and infinite and one and all alike. And it cannot perish or become greater, nor does it suffer pain or grief... .[11]

Melissus arrives at this astonishing idea by the same concept of changelessness which was seemingly a problem for Eddy's system earlier in this chapter; if any of these things happened to it, it would no longer be one.

> For if it is altered, then the real must needs [sic] not be all alike, but what was before must pass away, and what was not must come into being. ... Nor does it suffer pain; for a thing in pain could not all be. For a thing in pain could not be ever [sic], nor has it the same power as what is whole. Nor would it be alike, if it were in pain: for it is only from the addition or subtraction of something that it could feel pain, and then it would no longer be alike [i.e. no longer be the same, implying change, which is not possible, since an infinite entity could only change by becoming greater – which is impossible by definition – or by becoming nothing, which is also impossible].[12]

The same argument applies to grief as well as to pain. Consider the next part with reference to Eddy's concepts of spiritual sense versus the physical 'senses':

> Things... cannot be changed or altered, but each must be just as it is. ... Yet we fancy that they all suffer alteration, and they change from what we see each time. It is clear, then, that we do not see aright [sic] after all... They would

---

11. Burnet 1920, p. 321.
12. Ibid., pp. 321-22.

not change if they were real, but each thing would be as we believed it to be.[13]

The first extraordinary facet of Melissus' conclusion is not just its similarity with Eddy's but that he arrives at it without claiming the existence of God or gods. Eddy, on the other hand, requires God to exist for her entire argument to work, so we end up at the same point either way. Secondly, although a healing in Christian Science appears to cause a change in an individual, it is really only revealing the underlying truth that the patient was not ill in the first place. This is therefore another point of agreement between Melissus and Eddy.

J.M.E. McTaggart

The next comparison to make between the work of a respected philosopher and that of Eddy is that concerning John McTaggart Ellis McTaggart (1866-1925). McTaggart was a Cambridge idealist metaphysician, and amongst the most notable of the British idealists. Best known for 'The Unreality of Time'[14], in which, unsurprisingly, he argues that time is unreal, his work has been extensively discussed throughout the twentieth century and into the twenty-first.

McTaggart inherited from his predecessors an absolute commitment to the idea that a priori thought can pursue the nature of the ultimate reality, and, beyond this, is the *only* way to do so. For him, as with other Hegelians, this was the 'absolute idea'. His later work and mature system is mostly an attempt to give greater depth to this new conception of the absolute.

The reason for the focus on McTaggart at this point in the book is because he ultimately (after a meticulously detailed argument expressed with superlative clarity) arrived at some of the same conclusions as Eddy. There is a very intriguing difference, however, in the sequence of his argument. Eddy quickly arrives at the idea that the material universe is unreal, whereas McTaggart, after a lengthy proof that time is unreal, argues from this point that space is unreal, and as this eliminates the possibility of extension, matter must be unreal too. This process took McTaggart several tens of thousands of words, whereas Eddy arrived at the same result after just a single chapter of *Science and Health*.

---

13. Ibid., p. 322.
14. McTaggart 1908.

McTaggart's paradox

McTaggart's proof that the concept of time is self-contradictory implies that reality cannot therefore be temporal, with the consequence that the perception of time is therefore an illusion. His argument, known as McTaggart's paradox, first appeared as his journal article entitled 'The Unreality of Time', and was later republished as Chapter 33, 'Time', in McTaggart's posthumous second volume of *The Nature of Existence* in 1927. In it, he introduced the notions of the 'A series' and 'B series', representing two approaches to defining how events appear to have a position in time. The A series refers to the ideas of past, present and future, and is 'the series of positions running from the far past through the near past to the present, and then from the present to the near future and the far future'[15]. The B series, however, consists of positions ordered in a fixed manner, with interrelationships based on 'earlier-than' and 'later-than' descriptions. The A series, therefore, represents the events in 'time' to a temporally moving observer, whereas the B series is invariant.

McTaggart argued that the A series was a necessary component of all possible theories in which the existence of time is asserted, since change only occurs in the A series, but claimed that as this is self-contradictory, the perception of time must be illusory, as it is an incoherent concept.

The necessity of the A series

The first part of McTaggart's argument is his answer to the question 'whether it is essential to the reality of time that its events should form an A series as well as a B series'[16]. Essentially, McTaggart argues that events must be ordered by an A series as well as a B series as without this, change cannot exist, and so time becomes meaningless. Paraphrasing his argument, an example involving the births of Queen Victoria (b. 1818) and Queen Matilda (wife of Henry I, b. 1080) is instructive. The event of Queen Victoria's birth is a later event than the birth of Queen Matilda, and this property is invariant with 'time'; the events themselves also do not change. There is only one respect in which the events ever change:

---

15. McTaggart 1908, p. 458.
16. McTaggart 1927, p. 458.

It began by being a future event. It became every moment an event in the nearer future. At last it was a present event. Then it became past, and will always remain so, though every moment it becomes further and further past. Thus we seem forced to the conclusion that all change is only a change in the characteristics imparted to events by their presence in the A series.[17]

The incoherence of the A series

McTaggart's proof of the incoherence of the A series (McTaggart 1927, pp. 468-69) appears in the original paper as a single part of a very much more sophisticated argument for this conclusion. He argues that the human perception of time is contradictory, as all events appear to exemplify all three of the properties of the A series, i.e., past, present and future. The self-evident response to this is that no event exemplifies all three at once, i.e., that no event is past, present, and future 'simultaneously'. A single event *is* present, *will have been* future, *will be* past; here there seems, equally self-evidently, no contradiction. However, McTaggart argues that this gives rise to infinite regress, because this approach requires the invoking of a second A series of future, present, and past in order to explain how the events of the first series are not simultaneous, creating the necessity for a third series, and so on ad infinitum. In McTaggart's own words, it is necessary to construct 'a second A series, within which the first falls, in the same way in which events fall within the first' (ibid., p. 469), but the idea of a second A series within it will face the same contradiction, requiring the creation of a third A series within which the second series exists. This, of course, requires a fourth A series, and so on, ad infinitum. At every stage the contradiction will reappear; each A series will be, without reference to a further A series containing it, contradictory. McTaggart therefore concluded that the A series is inherently self-contradictory and, therefore cannot exist.

In *The Nature of Existence* (McTaggart 1921, 1927), McTaggart developed his own, highly original, metaphysical system, offering a Hegelian view of the universe consistent with his earlier work yet profoundly metaphysical throughout. McTaggart asserted that the world is composed of nothing of but love and souls, with each soul

---

17. Ibid., p. 460.

coupled to a number of the others by love. McTaggart claimed that souls (which are synonymous with human beings) are immortal, and, partly on this basis, defended the concept of reincarnation, maintaining the view that all selves are eternal and indestructible. *The Nature of Existence* also seeks to justify McTaggart's denial of the existence of time, space and matter despite their apparent existence. Conceptually linking with this work with Eddy is the combination of apparently mystical conclusions denying the reality of a conventionally unquestioned facet of existence, yet resulting from deductive logic. For example, although mystical in style when assessed by its conclusions, the philosophical methodology of *The Nature of Existence* is curiously unmystical. McTaggart arrives at his conclusions by a meticulous analysis of the fundamental requirements of all metaphysical systems (Volume I), followed by a proof that his system uniquely satisfies these conditions (Volume II). Logical rigour is central to his approach; *The Nature of Existence*, in conjunction with Bradley's *Appearance and Reality*, can be considered as the zenith of British idealism, with McTaggart being the last major British idealist of the period before the rise of logical positivism.

McTaggart points out that 'The Unreality of Time' is an inquiry into whether reality can have the characteristics which it appears to have, principally whether it is temporal and physically material. In the introduction to the second volume of *The Nature of Existence*, he states:

> Starting from our conclusions as to the general nature of the existent, as reached in the earlier Books, we shall have to ask, firstly which of these characteristics can really be possessed by what is existent, and which of them, despite the prima facie appearance to the contrary, cannot be possessed by anything existent.[18]

A little later, he adds that:

> It will be possible to show that, having regard to the general nature of the existent as previously determined, certain

---

18. McTaggart 1927, §295, p. 3.

characteristics, that we consider here for the first time, cannot be true of the existent.[19]

The most important result of McTaggart's inquiry into Absolute Reality, an inquiry using solely a priori arguments, is that existence and reality are equivalent and have no degrees of distinction: either something exists and therefore is fully real, or it does not, implying that for the future and past to be real, they must exist. Consequently, any future event or past event, even if they are the same event, must both exist if they are real, which is self-contradictory.

The C series

Having come to the conclusion that reality can form neither an A nor a B series, despite appearances to the contrary, then McTaggart offered a picture of what the world is really like, called the C series, describing it in great detail in *The Nature of Existence*[20]. Fundamentally, the C series consists of mental states (as McTaggart's argument in Chapter 34 of *The Nature of Existence* demonstrates that reality cannot be material), which are interrelated with each other on the basis of their conceptual content being either 'included-in' or 'inclusive-of'[21]. These atemporal relations replace the earlier-than/later-than relation and explain why the illusion of change and temporal sequences can appear to be present in an atemporal reality.

Here we see two very important isomorphisms with Eddy's earlier work: firstly, the recognition of the part played by illusion; and secondly, the demonstration of the non-material nature of reality. What follows is a heavily edited subset of McTaggart's arguments for the above concepts in note form, but nevertheless largely in his own words where possible:

> The first question which we must consider is whether it is essential to the reality of time that events should form an A series as well as a B series. It is clear, to begin with, that, in present experience, we never *observe* [original italics] events in time except as forming both these series.

---

19. Ibid., §298, p. 4.
20. McTaggart 1927: Chapters 44-49, pp. 193-255.
21. Ibid.: §566 and Chapter 60, p. 240 and pp. 355-64.

> We perceive events in time as being present, and those are the only events which we actually perceive. And all other events which, by memory or by inference, we believe to be real, we regard as present, past, or future. Thus the events of time as observed by us form an A series.[22]

McTaggart rejects this idea on the basis that the A series is essential to the nature of time, and asserts that regarding the A series as unreal is equal to treating time as unreal. McTaggart states that:

> [It is] universally admitted that time involves change... But there could be no time if nothing changed. ... If event N is ever earlier than event O and later than M, it will always be, and has always been, earlier than O and later than M, since the relations of earlier and later are permanent. N will thus always be in a B series.[23]

However, this absence of change is precisely what is needed as one step in the argument proving the unreality of time. Events in the A series are fixed within that series. Change does not take place to an object, but to its characteristics, which although they may be different, are attributable to each occurrence of that object in the A series; change does not occur to the object itself. In one respect only, it does change, in that it was once an event in the future, then at every moment an event in an ever-nearing future before, for an infinitesimal instant, becoming present, and then continuously receding into an ever more distant past.

McTaggart also explains that:

> This description of time is believed by most people, yet it clearly implies that the past is constantly changing, rather than fixed, as the same people believe; a combination which is inconsistent. The B series cannot exist except as temporal, since all its elements are interrelated by the terms 'earlier' and 'later', which are clearly time relations. It therefore follows that there can be no B series without an A series, as without an A series there is no such thing as time,

---

22. Ibid., §307, p. 11.
23. Ibid., pp. 11, 12.

and as there cannot be an A series either, as demonstrated earlier, time is therefore 'unreal'.[24]

And regarding matter:

> The world, in which we tend *primâ facie* to believe, is not, as is often said, divided into spirit and matter, but into spirit, sensa and matter. But we have found reason... to conclude that this *primâ facie* appearance was illusory in the case of matter, and that matter does not really exist. ... I propose to argue that the appearance is also illusory in the case of sensa... The object which we perceive has not the nature which it appears to have. ... I shall endeavour to show... that *the objects which we do perceive when we appear to appear sensa are all spiritual.* [my italics][25]

And even more explicitly:

> We shall conclude that sensa do not exist, though *other percepta are misperceived as sensa.* [my italics][26]

Extraordinary! Eddy herself could have written this last line, as it is one of the principles at the heart of Christian Science. In her case, publication occurred in 1875, four-and-a-half decades before McTaggart's date of publication. McTaggart concludes that we are certainly timeless, and therefore immortal, in the sense that there is no moment at which we shall cease to exist. Spinoza reached also reached this conclusion, and it is his work on this idea that I now wish to consider in relation to Eddy's.

Baruch Spinoza

Spinoza is one of the most important and most radical philosophers of the early modern period. His thought combines Cartesian metaphysical and epistemological principles with elements from Stoicism, Hobbes and his own ideas in an original system.

On God begins with Spinoza's definition of terms:

---

24. Ibid., p. 13.
25. Ibid., p. 57.
26. Ibid., p. xi.

1. By substance I understand what is in itself and is conceived through itself; 2. By attribute I understand what the intellect perceives of a substance, as constituting its essence; 3. By God I understand a being absolutely infinite, i.e., a substance consisting of an infinity of attributes, of which each one expresses an eternal and infinite essence.[27]

The definitions of *Part One* are the concepts that are foundational to the rest of his system. They are followed by a number of axioms that, he assumes, will be regarded as obvious and unproblematic by the philosophically informed ('Whatever is, is either in itself or in another'; 'From a given determinate cause the effect follows necessarily'). From these, the first proposition necessarily follows, and every subsequent proposition can be demonstrated using only what precedes it. In propositions one through fifteen of *Part One*, Spinoza presents the basic elements of his picture of God. God is the infinite, necessarily existing (that is, uncaused), unique substance of the universe. There is only one substance in the universe; it is God; and everything else that is, is in God.

> *Proposition 1*: A substance is prior in nature to its affections.
> *Proposition 2*: Two substances having different attributes have nothing in common with one another. (In other words, if two substances differ in nature, then they have nothing in common).
> *Proposition 3*: If things have nothing in common with one another, one of them cannot be the cause of the other.
> *Proposition 4*: Two or more distinct things are distinguished from one another, either by a difference in the attributes [i.e., the natures or essences] of the substances or by a difference in their affections [i.e., their accidental properties].
> *Proposition 5*: In nature, there cannot be two or more substances of the same nature or attribute.
> *Proposition 6*: One substance cannot be produced by another substance.
> *Proposition 7*: It pertains to the nature of a substance to exist.
> *Proposition 8*: Every substance is necessarily infinite.

---

27. Nadler 2024.

Proposition 9: The more reality or being each thing has, the more attributes belong to it.

Proposition 10: Each attribute of a substance must be conceived through itself.

Proposition 11: God, or a substance consisting of infinite attributes, each of which expresses eternal and infinite essence, necessarily exists. [The proof of this proposition is effectively that of the classic 'ontological proof for God's existence'. Spinoza writes that 'if you deny this, conceive, if you can, that God does not exist. Therefore, by Axiom 7… his essence does not involve existence. But this, by Proposition 7, is absurd. Therefore, God necessarily exists, QED.']

Proposition 12: No attribute of a substance can be truly conceived from which it follows that the substance can be divided.

Proposition 13: A substance which is absolutely infinite is indivisible.

Proposition 14: Except God, no substance can be or be conceived.[28]

The following are propositions edited from the translation by R. H. M. Elwes of Spinoza's *Ethics:*

PROP. I. Substance is by nature prior to its modifications.

PROP. II. Two substances, whose attributes are different, have nothing in common.

PROP. III. Things which have nothing in common cannot be one the cause of the

PROP. IV. Two or more distinct things are distinguished one from the other, either by the difference of the attributes of the substances, or by the difference of their modifications.

PROP. V. There cannot exist in the universe two or more substances having the same nature or attribute.

PROP. VI. One substance cannot be produced by another substance.

PROP. VII. Existence belongs to the nature of substances.

PROP. VIII. Every substance is necessarily infinite.

---

28. Nadler 2024.

PROP. IX. The more reality or being a thing has, the greater the number of its attributes.

PROP. X. Each particular attribute of the one substance must be conceived through itself.

PROP. XI. God, or substance, consisting of infinite attributes, of which each expresses eternal and infinite essentiality, necessarily exists.

PROP. XII. No attribute of substance can be conceived from which it would follow that substance can be divided.

PROP. XIII. Substance absolutely infinite is indivisible.

PROP. XIV. Besides God no substance can be granted or conceived.

PROP. XV. Whatsoever is, is in God, and without God nothing can be, or be conceived.

Proof.—Besides God, no substance is granted or can be conceived (by Prop. xiv.), that is nothing which is in itself and is conceived through itself. But modes can neither be, nor be conceived without substance; wherefore they can only be in the divine nature, and can only through it be conceived. But substances and modes form the sum total of existence, therefore, without God nothing can be, or be conceived. Q.E.D.

Although this approach to beginning the promulgation of a system of thought dates back at least as far as Euclid (and possibly very much earlier), there is much more of interest here than a merely surface similarity of method. Both Spinoza and Eddy are working towards the ultimate presentation of profoundly counterintuitive concepts, and so both begin by establishing an exceptionally detailed foundation for what comes later. As with Eddy, this work follows the structure of a presentation of a small number of fundamental propositions, followed by the deduction of a further principles, before investigating some of their real-world consequences.

Some annotation of Spinoza's list of propositions is needed here. Proposition 6, 'One substance cannot be produced by another substance' is clearly not the position of either chemistry or nuclear physics, but was an accepted principle at the time Spinoza was writing. Proposition 9 is wholly unlike McTaggart's assertion that a thing either exists, or it does not, with no 'levels' of reality, Proposition

10 makes the distinction between properties of an object requiring a subject, such as (for example) its odour requiring the presence of a subject experiencing that odour, and (again, for example) the number of legs possessed by a given animal, which is an independently true fact.

The proof that God – an infinite, necessary and uncaused, indivisible being – is the only substance of the universe involves three stages. Firstly, establish that no two substances can share an attribute or essence. Secondly, prove that there is a substance with infinite attributes (i.e., God). Thirdly, demonstrate that the existence of that infinite substance precludes the existence of any other substance. If there were to be a second substance, it would have to have some attribute or essence, but since God has all possible attributes, then the attribute to be possessed by this second substance would be one of the attributes already possessed by God, and as it has already been proved that no two substances can have the same attribute, it therefore follows that there can be, besides God, no such second substance. If God is the only substance, and whatever is, is either a substance or in a substance, then everything else must be in God. 'Whatever is, is in God, and nothing can be or be conceived without God'. Those things that are 'in' God (or, more precisely, in God's attributes) are what Spinoza calls modes. Here we see complete agreement between Spinoza and Eddy; more than this, the conclusion results from very similar arguments in each case.

By illuminating where there are similarities between Spinoza and Eddy's arguments and conclusions, I seek to demonstrate Eddy's true status as a philosopher, and by showing the sometimes profound differences in Eddy's conclusions with respect to Spinoza's, I aim to present the case for Eddy to be seen additionally as a highly original philosopher. Spinoza, like Eddy, asserts that God is substance and that everything is 'in' God. Spinoza claims that stones, furniture, animals, geomorphology and human beings are all 'properties' of God. It may appear counterintuitive to think that objects and individuals, i.e. independent 'things', are really merely properties of another thing.

Spinoza was aware of the alien nature of this idea, and of the philosophical problems which it creates. For Spinoza, pain and sickness are real. When a person feels pain, does it follow that the pain is ultimately just a property of God, and thus that God feels pain? Spinoza dealt with many issues raised, here and elsewhere, by asserting that God is described not so much as the underlying substance of all things, but as the universal, immanent and sustaining *cause* of all that exists:

> From the necessity of the divine nature there must follow infinitely many things in infinitely many modes, (i.e., everything that can fall under an infinite intellect).[29]

The infinite and finite modes are not just effects of God or Nature's power but actually inhere in that infinite substance. Nature is an indivisible, uncaused, substantial whole – in fact, it is the *only* substantial whole. Outside of Nature, there is nothing, and everything that exists is a part of Nature and is brought into being by Nature with a deterministic necessity. This unified, unique, productive, necessary being just is what is meant by 'God'.

Although the majority of this is extremely similar to Eddy's system of thought, one aspect is diametrically opposite. Where Spinoza refers to Nature (which he capitalises) he is signifying a physically extant reality, similar to, but not exactly the same as, what our sensory perception suggests it to be. Eddy, however, denies its existence entirely, substituting a spiritual reality which is sometimes in close correspondence with the beliefs created by what we misidentify as our physical 'senses', but at other times wholly different to them.

Spinoza has been regarded as a pantheist. However, in general, pantheism is the view that rejects the transcendence of God. According to pantheism, God is, in some way, identical with the world, although there may be aspects of God that are ontologically or epistemologically distinct from the world, but for pantheism this must not imply that God is essentially separate from the world. Within this generic definition, it is possible to delineate two types of pantheism. Firstly, pantheism can be understood as the denial of any distinction whatsoever between God and the natural world and the assertion that God is in fact identical with everything that exists: 'God is everything and everything is God' (Fox quoted in Ingle 1996. In this view, God is the world and all its natural contents, and nothing distinct from them; this has been termed 'reductive' pantheism. Secondly, pantheism can be defined as the position asserting that God is distinct from the world and its natural contents but nonetheless contained or immanent *within* them. God is therefore still everything and everywhere in this

---

29. Nadler 2024.

form of pantheism, in this version, by virtue of being within everything. This is known as 'immanentist' pantheism and involves the claim that nature contains within itself, in addition to its natural elements, an immanent, supernatural and divine element.

Eddy faced repeated accusations from a variety of critics that Christian Science is pantheistic, something which she both rejected and found bitterly unjust, as, from her viewpoint, the established Churches were occasionally guilty of an element of pantheism, whereas she maintained that Christian Science was absolutely its opposite. In 1898 she published *Christian Science versus Pantheism* (Eddy 1898), which expresses the difference so clearly and completely that, in order to do both it and Christian Science justice, I would like to present a lengthy quote from it:

> The Standard Dictionary has it that pantheism is the doctrine of the deification of natural causes, conceived as one personified nature, to which the religious sentiment is directed. Theism is the belief in the personality and infinite mind of one supreme, holy, self-existent God, who reveals Himself supernaturally to His creation, and whose laws are not reckoned as science. In religion, it is a belief in one God, or in many gods. It is opposed to atheism and monotheism, but agrees with certain forms of pantheism and polytheism. It is the doctrine that the universe owes its origin and continuity to the reason, intellect, and will of a self-existent divine Being, who possesses all wisdom, goodness, and power, and is the creator and preserver of man. God, Spirit, is indeed the preserver of man. ... This being the case, what need have we of drugs, hygiene, and medical therapeutics, if these are not man's preservers? By admitting self-evident affirmations and then contradicting them, monotheism is lost and pantheism is found in scholastic theology. Can a single quality of God, Spirit, be discovered in matter? The Scriptures plainly declare, 'The Word was God;' and 'all things were made by Him,' – the Word. What, then, can matter create, or how can it exist? It is plain that elevating evil to the altitude of mind gives it power, and that the belief in more than one spirit, if Spirit, God, is infinite, breaketh the First Commandment in the Decalogue. Again: The hypothesis of mind in matter, or

more than one Mind, lapses into evil dominating good, matter governing Mind, and makes sin, disease, and death inevitable, despite of Mind, or by the consent of Mind! ... They constantly reiterate the belief of pantheism, that mind 'sleeps in the mineral, dreams in the animal, and wakes in man.' Is there a religion under the sun that hath demonstrated one God and the four first rules pertaining thereto, namely, 'Thou shalt have no other gods before me;' 'Love thy neighbor as thyself;' 'Be ye therefore perfect, even as your Father which is in heaven is perfect;' 'Whosoever liveth and believeth in me shall never die.' (John xi. 26.)[30]

Eddy is suggesting here that conventional Christianity is arguably quasi-paganistic due to the idea that creation is separate to God, though God-made. As pagan religions are sometimes explicitly pantheistic, she is effectively pointing out that conventional Christianity risks the charge of pantheism, not based on a false understanding (as with those who accuse Christian Science of pantheism), but on one which may well be true!

An analysis of Spinoza's identification of God and Nature will clearly show that Spinoza cannot be considered to be a pantheist in the second, immanentist sense, since for Spinoza, there is nothing but Nature and its attributes and 'modes'. And within Nature there can certainly be nothing that is supernatural; if Spinoza is attempting to eliminate anything, it is that which is above or beyond nature (i.e. which is unencumbered by the laws and processes of nature). However, the question remains as to whether he is a pantheist in the first, reductive sense.

It can be argued that Spinoza is not a pantheist, because God is to be identified only with substance and its attributes, the most universal, active causal principles of Nature, and not with any modes of substance. Alternatively, others have argued that Spinoza is a pantheist because he does identify God with the whole of Nature. However, if 'pantheism' is meant to represent the idea that God is everything, and if one reads Spinoza as saying that God is only *Natura naturans*, then Spinoza's God is not everything and consequently he is not a pantheist.

---

30. Eddy 1898, pp. 2-3.

Finite things, on this reading, while caused by the eternal, necessary and active aspects of Nature, are not identical with God or substance, but rather are its effects. In fact, however the relationship between God and Nature in Spinoza is interpreted, it is a mistake to call him a pantheist in so far as pantheism is a type of religious theism. The pantheist asserts that God – conceived as a being before which one is to adopt an attitude of worshipful awe – is or is in Nature; Spinoza does not believe that worship, awe or reverence is appropriate in considering either God or Nature. There is nothing holy or sacred about Nature, and it is certainly not the object of a religious experience. Instead, one should seek to understand God or Nature with the intellectual knowledge that reveals Nature's most important truths and which demonstrates how everything depends essentially and existentially on higher natural causes.

The key to discovering and experiencing God, for Spinoza, is philosophy and science. Superstitious behaviour and subservience to ecclesiastic authorities is, for Spinoza, the exact opposite. Apart from the use of the word 'science', which both Spinoza and Eddy use in its modern sense, this is absolutely at odds with Eddy's conception of existence, for if all that exists is Spirit, and Spirit is quite literally synonymous with God (as it is within her 'scientific definition'), then awe and worship are exactly what is appropriate and required of mankind.

There is, for Spinoza, no causal interaction between bodies and ideas, between the physical and the mental. There is, however, a strong correlation and isomorphism between the two series. One of the greatest questions in seventeenth-century philosophy was the problem of how two radically different substances such as mind and body enter into a union in a human being and cause effects in each other. How can the extended body causally interact with the unextended mind, which is incapable of contact or motion, and 'move' it, that is, cause generic mental consequences, such as pains, sensations and perceptions. Spinoza, however, denies that human beings are the union of two substances. The human mind and the human body are two different expressions – under thought and under extension – of one and the same thing, the person; since there is no causal interaction between the mind and the body, the so-called mind-body problem does not arise.

Eddy, of course, eliminates the mind-body problem by denying the physical existence of the body. In as much as we have bodies, for Eddy they are formed from the same 'spirit' as is mind, so no such problem can exist. As everything is in a sense within God, God – Spirit – is for Eddy the ultimate source of all action, which is a similar approach regarding causality to that of Malebranche, and it is this facet of the latter's philosophy I now wish to explore.

Nicolas Malebranche

The French Cartesian Nicolas Malebranche published major works on metaphysics, theology, and ethics (as well as studies within 'natural philosophy', such as on optics, the laws of motion and the nature of colour), but is known for his original synthesis of the ideas of St Augustine and Descartes. Two profoundly distinctive results of this synthesis are Malebranche's doctrine that we see bodies as seen through ideas in God and his occasionalist conclusion that God is the only real cause (Malebranche Œuvres complètes, 2:316 in the Robinet edition 1958).

Despite the neglect of him in the Anglophone literature during the majority of the twentieth century, Malebranche has become increasingly popular as an area of research among English-language academics more recently. This change is visible in the number of English translations of his writings since the 1970s, and particularly since the 1990s. Fairly recent studies of Malebranche in English include Walton (1972), Radner (1978), McCracken (1983), Jolley (1990), Nadler (1992), Schmaltz (1996), Nadler (2000), Pyle (2003), and Peppers-Bates (2009).

In a section of the third book of the *Recherche*[31] devoted to 'the nature of ideas', Malebranche argued for his distinctive doctrine of the vision in God. The concept in this section is that external objects are seen by means of ideas in God, the argument for which is as follows. It begins with the assertion that:

> 'everyone agrees that we do not perceive objects external to us by themselves' since it cannot be true that 'the soul should leave the body to stroll about the heavens to see the objects present there'.[32]

---

31. Malebranche 1980c.
32. Enfield 1791, p. 619.

Malebranche claimed that there that only four other possibilities if the concept that bodies are perceived through ideas in God is rejected, three of which are immediately contradictory, leaving the hypothesis that:

> Our soul perceives the essence and the existence of bodies by the consideration of its own set of perfections.[33]

Malebranche's argument against the fourth hypothesis begins with the observation that since a finite being can see in itself neither the infinite nor an infinite number of beings, and since we in fact perceive both the infinite and infinity in external objects, it must be that we see these objects by means of perfections contained in the only being that can possess an infinity of ideas, which in turn must, of course, be God.

Malebranche is best known for the concept of occasionalism, i.e., that God is the only causal agent, and beings simply strive to provide the 'occasion' for divine action (Malebranche *Œuvres complètes*, 2:316 in the Robinet edition 1958). Malebranche used this approach in order to resolve the problem with Cartesian dualism. Previously, occasionalists had conceded that God must 'concur' with creatures in producing effects, but claimed that there is reason to conclude that creatures are true secondary causes of effects; if not, there could be no true scientific explanation of effects through their natural causes, the desire to retain this approach to explanation presumably outweighing the self-evident logic. Malebranche responded to arguments against 'pure' occasionalism by asserting that it is in reality idolatrous to attribute divine power to creatures, rather as Eddy explicitly stated in relation to attributing any power to matter. Malebranche's argument that only God can produce effects is predicated upon the concept that 'a true cause… is one such that the mind perceives a necessary connection between it and its effects'[34]. As no such connection exists within bodily states, between bodily and mental states, or even within purely mental states, the only causal connection must be between an omnipotent Deity's volitions and the divine will.

---

33. Ibid., p. 619.
34. Enfield 1791, pp. 618 ff.

Theodicy

The existence of evil is problematic for any system of thought which claims that the world was created by a God who has infinite power, knowledge and goodness. However, the problem is a profoundly difficult one for occasionalism, as here only God is the cause of all effects in nature. Malebranche's theodicy addresses the problem of evil by admitting that God could have acted to prevent natural evils such as illness, and thus could have produced a more perfect world, but that God could have created a more perfect world only by sacrificing the simplicity and uniformity of action that is a supreme mark of His wisdom. God therefore does not will those specific evils, but they arise because He wills a world governed by the fewest laws.

Although an ingenious argument, it does not serve to explain why God does not will a universe with the fewest laws which would still completely eliminate the existence of evil. Evil therefore remains a severe difficulty for Malebranche, whereas for Eddy it is quite literally no problem at all, as within her system, evil doesn't exist. Consequently, despite the radically counterintuitive nature of Christian Science, it is less problematic, and therefore easier to accept as a system.

Julian of Norwich

Another writer whose conclusions concur with those of Eddy and McTaggart, yet who offers a third methodology in so doing, is the first woman ever to publish a book written in English, the anchorite Julian of Norwich. In a series of sixteen visions, which she termed as 'showings', Julian believed that the essential character of God had been revealed to her, and after considerable reflective analysis of these showings, she concluded that the ultimate reality consists of solely of God's love.

Philip Sheldrake conducted a detailed analysis of the work of Julian of Norwich, in which he explained that 'The visions are simply starting points for her teaching about God's love for humanity'[35] and, furthermore, that:

---

35. Sheldrake 2018, p. 85.

Our ignorance of God's love keeps us in sin and despair. In the end, therefore, there is only one 'showing' or 'revelation', and that is God's love as the meaning of everything.[36]

This serves as an introduction to the explanation of the use of the word 'love' in this context: 'God's love is not an emotion. Nor is it one characteristic of God or simply related to God's external action. For Julian, love is God's very being or reality'[37]. Julian herself expands upon this idea, providing the following detail:

Know it well, love was his meaning. Who reveals it to you? Love. Why does he reveal it to you? For love. Remain in this and you will know more of the same. But you will never know different, without end. So I was taught that love is our Lord's meaning.[38]

Sheldrake then explains that:

Love is… the whole teaching of Julian's book. Everything else (including, for example, God's Lordship) is to be interpreted in the light of love. God may be thought of as all-powerful and all-knowing, but the deepest truth about God is love.[39]

For Julian, God is not just all of creation, but also all of action: 'See, I am God. See, I do all things. See, I never remove my hands from my works, nor ever shall, without end'[40]. Love, however, she considered as something quite different: 'Love is not something God "does" or "has". Rather, love is God's very nature and this love is directed outwards towards… humanity in particular'[41].

---

36. Sheldrake 2018, p. 84.
37. Ibid., p. 86.
38. Quoted, ibid., p. 91.
39. Ibid., p. 92.
40. Quoted, Ibid., p. 104.
41. Quoted, Ibid., p. 110.

This she made clear in her 'showing':

> And I saw no difference between God and our substance, but, as it were, all God; and still my understanding accepted that our substance is in God, that is to say that God is God, and our substance is a creature of God. For the almighty truth of the Trinity is our Father, for he made us and keeps us in him. And the deep wisdom of the Trinity is our Mother, in whom we are enclosed. And the goodness of the Trinity is our Lord, and in him we are enclosed and he is in us. We are enclosed in the Father, and we are enclosed in the Son, and we are enclosed in the Holy Spirit, and the Holy Spirit is enclosed in us, almighty, all wisdom and all goodness, one God, one Lord.[42]

Thus we have the same conclusion by whether deduction from initially a priori axioms which are subsequently justified empirically, in Eddy's case, deduction from a priori principles which remain a priori, in McTaggart's case, and reflection upon revelation, in the case of Julian of Norwich.

Extreme criticism in the twenty-first century

Gerald Bergmann, writing in 2001, described Eddy's system of thought as itself 'delusional'. In an essay with the intensely provocative title *The Christian Science Holocaust* (Bergmann 2001) he sought to dismantle Christian Science, starting with its initial axioms, and progressing to the ideas arriving from them. Perhaps Bergmann was unaware that these criticisms of Eddy are not original, having been made by Farnsworth (and many others) roughly a century before[43]. Given Eddy's zealousness in defending what she referred to as her 'discovery', it is unsurprising that she published responses to these and other more sophisticated criticisms[44]. For example, as quoted earlier:

> If I have the toothache, and nothing stops it until I have the tooth extracted, and then the pain ceases, has the

---

42. Quoted, Ibid., p. 112.
43. Farnsworth 1909.
44. Eddy 1897, p. 45.

mind, or extracting, or both, caused the pain to cease? What you thought was pain in the bone or nerve, could only have been a belief of pain in matter; for matter has no sensation. It was a state of mortal thought made manifest in the flesh. You call this body matter, when awake, or when asleep in a dream. That matter can report pain, or that mind *is in* matter, reporting sensations, is but a dream at all times. You believed that if the tooth were extracted, the pain would cease: this demand of mortal thought once met, your belief assumed a new form, and said, There is no more pain. When your belief in pain ceases, the pain stops; for matter has no intelligence of its own. By applying this mental remedy or antidote directly to your belief, you scientifically prove the fact that Mind is supreme.[45]

Criticisms of Bergmann's form (i.e. that Eddy was delusional) are from the point of view of a materialist interpreting 'sensory data' regarding a physical world as providing the basis for its existence. Having 'proved' this hypothesis, any idealist alternative – any *whatsoever*, whether Eddy's or not – is, therefore, from this standpoint delusional, but this is really simply a restatement of the initial physicalist premise. Exactly the same structure of argument could be used with idealism as its premise, with the conclusion being – again, in the absence of evidence – that belief in the physicalist world is delusional. It is said that 'familiarity breeds contempt'; perhaps, in the case of Christian Science, it is the lack of familiarity which publishes contempt.

Conclusion

Although there are clearly some problematic aspects to Mary Baker Eddy's system of thought, it is nevertheless a tour de force worthy of much greater analytical interest than was the case during the twentieth century. In echoing the ideas of earlier thinkers such as Spinoza and Malebranche, who are undoubtedly regarded as being philosophers, Eddy must be redefined as a philosopher, despite her protestations regarding '99% of philosophy'. Furthermore, her sometimes profound yet evidenced disagreements with the

---

45. Eddy 1897, pp. 44-45.

ideas of these thinkers, coupled with publishing ideas isomorphic to McTaggart's, but 52 years before him, means that she must additionally be regarded as a genuinely original philosopher. In fact, her originality abounds: methodological contributions, her concept of God as Father-Mother, her thoroughgoing idealism, her concept of spiritual sense, her redefinitions of many existing terms in theology and philosophy and her dazzling denials of so much that is 'common sense' – all this points to a creative and daring intellect.

As has been demonstrated, Eddy's system of thought has been misrepresented by many authors, and additionally faced criticism based on a myriad of different misunderstandings. Recent world events have created the possibility of this unfortunate situation reoccurring; the next chapter therefore addresses this issue.

Chapter 9

Criticism and Controversy

The Spanish Influenza and the COVID-19 Pandemic

Background to the events

This chapter explores the important dichotomy between what would be Eddy's denial of the existence of SARS-CoV 2 as a specific pathogen within her denial of the existence of all illnesses, and the unitary denial of COVID-19 by various subgroups in twenty-first-century society whose world model is diametrically opposed to that of Christian Science.

The previous chapters have described Eddy's philosophical system in detail, so there is no need to repeat that level of analysis here, other than to restate a brief summary for the purpose of demonstrating the profound differences which exist between Eddy's philosophy and the assumptions and assertions of those who would describe themselves as COVID deniers. The parallels between the Christian Science understanding of Spanish Influenza and that of COVID-19 are particularly instructive in this regard. The 378-page book published in 1922 by the Christian Science Church on their response to the circumstances created by the Great War includes a substantial section on Spanish Influenza, and offers a very different viewpoint to that of the conventionally accepted one of *materia medica*. Given the once-in-a-century nature of the COVID-19 pandemic, I felt it important to consider this aspect, and especially so given Eddy's central claims. This chapter will therefore use the historic Christian Science philosophical response to Spanish Influenza as a source of information for the analysis of the new pandemic, and specifically how it might be misunderstood in relation to the twenty-first-century situation.

Given the overwhelming numbers of casualties due to the 1918-19 Influenza (estimated as being 50 million to 100 million worldwide), and the consequent fact that virtually every extended family would have lost someone to the virus, it might quite reasonably be thought that the Christian Science assertion regarding the nonexistence of illness could have proved hard to maintain during this historical period. The truth, however, is that, if anything, far from diluting or side-stepping this central claim, Christian Scientists were even more vociferous than usual. *The Christian Science Response in Wartime*[1] devotes much of its text to how Christian Scientists responded to Spanish Influenza. This is not surprising: far more people died of the 'flu pandemic than were killed in the Great War. Christian Scientists were not untouched themselves. How did they respond to a complex situation, the cause and extent of which were reported and debated in the press? How did their practice of spiritual healing contribute to alleviating the crisis?

Several aspects of their response stand out. The *Christian Science Monitor* covered the pandemic closely and editorialised on it. In 1919 the newspaper made this observation:

> If... the press could be induced to advertise courage instead of circulating fear, an enormous improvement would be rapidly manifested. The effect of the mere corralling of fear would be inestimable. The greatest service any paper, any doctor, any human being can perform for the human race is to teach it to think aright.[2]

The world model represented by Christian Science goes far beyond the denial of either influenza viruses or the existence of SARS-CoV 2,

---

1. Brock, Chalmers and Dickey 1922.
2. 'Architects of Disease', *The Christian Science Monitor*, 13 August 1919, p. 16.

the virus which scientists believe causes COVID-19. Eddy would of course deny the existence of COVID-19, but only on the basis that it is an example of the erroneously asserted entity known as 'illness'. It would therefore be an injustice to characterise Eddy as a 'COVID denier', despite the literal truth of the description, for at least nine different reasons. These will now be explored.

Firstly, and most fundamentally, completely different reasoning underpins her assertion. There is no reason to believe that COVID deniers are philosophical idealists. Their statements and behaviour strongly suggest complete commitment to a belief in physical existence, apart from that of COVID-19, of course. This is wholly antithetical to Eddy's position that entire physical world simply does not exist.

Secondly, there is no reason to believe that COVID deniers disbelieve in the existence of other illnesses; their assertions regarding SARS-CoV 2 and COVID-19 are specific to these and only these constructs. Again, this is very different to the position of Christian Science, which is that (i) no physically existent, pathogenic organisms exist, and (ii) no illnesses exist.

Thirdly, COVID deniers assert that a variety of governments, national institutions and multinational companies are involved in a global conspiracy which (i) fictitiously asserts the existence of COVID-19, and (ii) compels populations to accept what although termed vaccines are 'in reality' some unspecified form of control, often involving 'microchips'. Both of these core aspects – global conspiracy and maliciously injecting billions of citizens under false pretences – if true, would be undeniably examples of evil. Eddy, though, as an extremely early stage of her argument, concluded that 'evil' in any form whatsoever cannot possibly exist, and is merely the false belief in an erroneous human construct; a campaign involving harmful injections is therefore not possible within her world view.

Fourthly, the behaviour of some COVID deniers is aggressive, involving threats of physical violence, rape and death being made against medical and nursing professionals, and even their children, all on the basis of seeking to force the individuals concerned to 'admit' their part in the assumed conspiracy and desist from their alleged activities within it. As the term 'COVID denier' is inextricably associated with these behaviours and the many other views regarding the supposed 'true' purpose of vaccines, none of which would have been shared by Eddy, the potential injustice begins to appear.

Intriguingly, this particular aspect, being a form of 'evil' if – from Eddy's standpoint – it were to exist, clearly cannot do so; the apparent behaviour being illusory implies that, in the absence of this behaviour, the individuals concerned cease to be COVID deniers, and may of course be illusory themselves. Either way, Eddy would seem to be forced to deny the existence of COVID deniers!

The fifth difference between the beliefs of COVID deniers and Eddy's world model, following from the difference above, is that it is a reasonable assumption that COVID deniers do not deny their own existence!

Sixthly, resulting from her denial of the existence of physical reality, Eddy could not have concurred with the assertion that vaccines exist, irrespectively of their 'true' purpose; this is entirely separate from the assumed conspiracy held to exist by COVID deniers.

Seventhly, a very different further source of disparity between 'modern' COVID denial and the position arising from Christian Science relates to the published statistics regarding cases, hospitalisations and deaths from the disease. In this case, at first sight both sides appear to be in perfect agreement: they would both allege that no cases or deaths are occurring and the published figures are untrue. Again, however, the underlying reasons for these shared beliefs could hardly be more different; COVID deniers believe the statistics to be a malicious and intentional fiction, whereas from Eddy's point of view the figures are incorrect because death is an illusion.

Eighthly, the type of mathematical function which describes the published statistics regarding both Spanish Influenza and COVID-19 is known as an exponential function. As a consequence of the 2020 pandemic, this word is now often misused: it does not apply to a quantity and has no implication regarding size; instead, it refers to the *shape of the curve describing 'geometric' growth*. An example of this form is one with a constant ratio, such as the series 1, 2, 4, 8, 16… in which each term is twice the previous one. This is called natural growth, as biological systems, such as the spread of infections, display it due to the fact that each infected person goes on to infect a number of other people; if, for example, this number is two, then the series above is recreated. In the absence of a self-replicating organism or system, this pattern is unlikely to occur. Returning to the issue of COVID-19, the only way that the published figures for cases could follow geometric growth is if each case creates more than one new

Criticism and Controversy   151

case, i.e., in the presence of a contagious infection. Both modern COVID deniers and Eddy would agree that geometric growth could not be taking place, and both would point to the lack of an infective, contagious organism, but, aside from this context, Eddy's position would appear to rule out this form of growth under any circumstances. This is not simply because of her disbelief in either illness or the organisms associated with it, but because an exponential function is caused by the rate of growth of a system being dependent upon its absolute level, and it is difficult to envisage how this could be true within the profoundly idealist world view of Christian Science.

Ninthly, and finally, the conspiracy which COVID deniers allege is held by some of their number to be a component part of an older a far greater global conspiracy, sometimes known as the New World Order. This fundamentally atheistic, geopolitical project, were it to exist, would be diametrically opposed to Christian Science in seemingly every aspect, given that it would be non-idealist in conception, assert the nonexistence of God and be of malicious intent.

The Goat Island experiment

Despite its radical nature, Christian Science does not include any element of paranoia or conspiracy theorisation in its argument for the nonexistence of COVID-19. With regard to Spanish Influenza, the Christian Science religious periodicals also shared reports pointing to the deleterious effects of collective fear, to medical tests that called into question popular assumptions, and to acts of unselfishness and courage. For example, the 12 April 1919 *Christian Science Sentinel* reprinted this from California's *Oakland Enquirer*:

> The experiments made at Goat Island [California] by Navy doctors in an effort to learn something about the influenza germ, carry a lesson that every person should study and understand. Fifty young sailors volunteered to become influenza victims, that the doctors might study the disease more carefully. These young men had no fear of the disease; they willingly offered themselves. They were placed with flu patients; they were given jars of flu germs, which they breathed into their lungs; they had flu germs injected into their bodies. … But no cases developed among these fifty sailors! These men had been inoculated; they had been

exposed to the disease in every manner; they had breathed in the germs and eaten and slept with flu victims, and not one of them became infected! The medical men confessed themselves baffled. All their ideas of the disease were turned topsy-turvy. ... The doctors are still wondering. The explanation, however, is simplicity itself, for it was proved by each one of these fifty young men. These fifty young men volunteered to act as subjects upon which to be experimented. This showed clearly that they did not fear the disease.[3]

Referencing the Goat Island experiment, the *Journal of the American Medical Association* offered a frank observation:

Dr. McCoy, who with Dr. Richey, did a similar series of experiments on Goat Island, San Francisco, used volunteers, who, so far as known, had not been exposed to the outbreak at all, also had negative results, that is, they were unable to reproduce the disease. Perhaps there are factors, or a factor, in the transmission of influenza that we do not know.[4]

If false, this is clearly an extremely dangerous idea. That having been acknowledged, however, it is nevertheless a concept with some contemporary traction, with the work of Bruce Lipton being of particular importance. Despite having a PhD in biology, Lipton has made the case for a reconsideration of the germ theory of disease, noting the similarity between Eddy's claims and those reported by medical professionals long after her original publication. For example:

When the mind, through positive suggestion improves health, it is referred to as the placebo effect. Conversely, when the same mind is engaged in negative suggestions that can damage health, the negative effects are referred to as the *nocebo* effect. ... A Nashville physician, Clifton Meador... had a patient, Sam Londe, a retired shoe

---

3. *Christian Science Sentinel*, 12 April 1919, p. 637.
4. Rosenau 1919, p. 313.

salesman suffering from cancer of the esophagus, a condition that was at the time considered 100 per cent fatal. Londe was treated for that cancer but everyone in the medical community 'knew' that his esophageal cancer would recur. So it was no surprise when Londe died a few weeks after his diagnosis. The surprise came after Londe's death when an autopsy found very little cancer in his body, certainly not enough to kill him. There were a couple of spots in the liver and one in the lung, but there was no trace of the [o]esophageal cancer that everyone thought had killed him. ... What did Londe die of if not esophageal cancer? Had he died because he *believed* he was going to die? The case still haunts Meador three decades after Londe's death.[5]

Another quote is even more explicit:

[The] nineteenth century German physician Robert Koch, who along with Pasteur founded the Germ Theory, [which] holds that bacteria and viruses are the primary cause of disease. ... One of Koch's critics was so convinced that the germ theory was wrong that he brazenly wolfed down a glass of water laced with vibrio cholerae, the bacterium Koch believed caused cholera. To everyone's astonishment, the man was completely unaffected by the [supposedly] virulent pathogen.[6]

The patient survived, yet the 'unanimity of opinion on the Germ Theory'[7] was unchanged. Furthermore, physicians and biologists disregard this and other 'embarrassing "messy" exceptions that spoil their theories. ... The problem is that there cannot be exceptions to a theory; exceptions simply mean that a theory is not fully correct'[8].

But what of Christian Science treatments which do not result in the disappearance of symptoms? Isn't this an example of an exception

---

5. Lipton 2005, pp. 142-143.
6. Ibid., p. 126. Lipton cites DiRita 2000 as the source of this account.
7. Ibid., p. 126.
8. Ibid., p. 126.

meaning that Eddy's theory is not fully correct? This would be consistent with Lipton's argument, and presumably the opinion of the majority of the population who are not Christian Scientists (i.e. approximately 99.9987% of the world population, assuming it to be around eight billion and the number of Christian Scientists as roughly 100,000), but it neglects the involvement of the patient in exactly the way in which Lipton is arguing. In both cases, it is the patient's belief which is crucial to the presence or absence of 'illness'.

Debates at the time of the Spanish Influenza

During the pandemic, Protestant, Catholic and Jewish leaders debated government orders to close places of worship. Some believed that their ministry was needed more than ever, and that their doors should remain open. Christian Scientists participated in this debate; at least one branch Church tried to challenge a closure order, but its suit was refused. Christian Scientist volunteer workers regularly reported on their activities during this period, providing many accounts.

> There were also reports from enlisted men who were Christian Scientists: One of the things for which we are most grateful is the fact that our boys were able to help the others during the recent epidemic. One of them had charge of thirty-six others. The first night he went to each patient and tried to allay his fear and to reassure him. The doctors soon began to turn to him and he was put into a position of considerable responsibility and usefulness. Another boy read the 91st Psalm to his patients, and although only a beginner in Science, through using what he knew of the truth, was able to overcome a very high fever for one of the boys.[9]

Similarly, a soldier writing from England said:

> I was placed in a hospital unit and sent overseas. This took place while the fear of the… influenza was on. … If you will remember I am just a beginner in Science, and so I held to the truth as best I could during that season. I did not use

---

9. Brock, Chalmers and Dickey 1922, p. 342.

any preventives or medicine as did my associates. I had no fear and felt it my duty to serve instead of being served.[10]

Individual Christian Scientists all over the world faced their own challenges during the epidemic. Many testimonies published after 1919 in the *Sentinel* and *The Christian Science Journal,* and in the French and German editions of *The Herald of Christian Science,* mentioned healings of Spanish flu. As far as Christian Scientists were concerned, during the Spanish Influenza epidemic a great mass of evidence was accumulated showing the physical healings resulting from the application of Christian Science to the treatment of disease. Some of these healings were brought about by the ministrations of War Relief Workers, whereas others were by the efforts of soldier Scientists on their own behalf or on behalf of comrades. The testimonial which follows, from a Christian Scientist, is of this nature.

> As testimonial to the exceedingly good work a Christian Science Welfare Worker did for me I wish to relate my experience at Kelly Field, San Antonio, Texas....
>
> Last fall, during the 'flu' epidemic, I became suddenly ill. The day before I became unconscious, some Science literature was handed me, with the Welfare Worker's name enclosed. I refused medicine of any kind, and called on the Welfare Worker for help. The next day I was forcibly taken to the hospital and passed almost immediately into unconsciousness. The Welfare Worker was with me every day and several nights practically all night.
>
> It was at a critical stage, when the army surgeon at the hospital said I could not live until a certain hour. They had done absolutely all they could, and told my parents that I would probably be dead within a few hours. This condition lasted for over a day. The Worker brought me back into sunshine and life again, staying constantly with me.
>
> The case was considered a very peculiar one in the hospital, and the surgeon predicted all kinds of after effects, none of which developed, nor ever will, for this experience has shown me thoroughly what Science is and what it will do for one....

---

10. Ibid., p. 343.

William Huttig, Jr.,
Kansas City, Mo.[11]

This echoed Eddy's own prior practical experience, which is the reason for its inclusion at this point. Eddy's experiments and the results from specific 'healings' are considered next.

Eddy's own experiments

On the issue of contagious illness being caused by a virus, Eddy's assertion that matter does not exist of course implies that as well as the illness being an error of belief, so is the belief in the existence of the virus, the only 'contagion' being that of being exposed to the false beliefs. In *Science and Health* (Eddy 1910, pp. 153-57) Eddy describes her own experiences, using the term 'experiments', and, as before, implicitly using the sequence 'hypothesis, experiment, results, conclusion':

> The author's medical researches [*sic*] and experiments had prepared her thought for the metaphysics of Christian Science. Every material dependence had failed her in her search for truth; and she can now understand why, and can see the means by which mortals are divinely driven to a spiritual source for health and happiness. You say a boil is painful; but that is impossible, for matter without mind is not painful. The boil simply manifests, through inflammation and swelling, a belief in pain, and this belief is called a boil. Now administer mentally to your patient a high attenuation of truth, and it will soon cure the boil. The fact that pain cannot exist where there is no mortal mind to feel it is a proof that this so-called mind makes its own pain – that is, its own belief in pain. We weep because others weep, we yawn because they yawn, and we have smallpox because others have it; but mortal mind, not matter, contains and carries the infection. When this mental contagion is understood, we shall be more careful of our mental conditions and we shall avoid loquacious tattling

---

11. Ibid., p. 334.

> about disease, as we would avoid advocating crime. Neither sympathy nor society should ever tempt us to cherish error in any form, and certainly we should not be error's advocate. Disease arises, like other mental conditions, from association. Since it is a law of mortal mind that certain diseases should be regarded as contagious, this law obtains credit through association, – calling up the fear that creates the image of disease and its consequent manifestation in the body.[12]

Eddy then describes an extraordinarily unethical experiment (in which she was not involved). This is an interesting albeit shocking account:

> This fact in metaphysics is illustrated by the following incident: A man was made to believe that he occupied a bed where a cholera patient had died. Immediately the symptoms of this disease appeared, and the man died. The fact was, that he had not caught the cholera by material contact, because no cholera patient had been in that bed.[13]

Here, Eddy is discussing the nocebo effect, but then looks at the effect of belief more generally, considering that of the patient and the physician:

> When the sick recover by the use of drugs, it is the law of a general belief, culminating in individual faith, which heals; and according to this faith will the effect be. Even when you take away the individual confidence in the drug, you have not yet divorced the drug from the general faith. … When the general belief endorses the inanimate drug as doing this or that, individual dissent or faith, unless it rests on Science, is but a belief held by a minority, and such a belief… weighs against the high and mighty truths of Christian metaphysics… The percentage of power on the side of this Science must mightily outweigh the power of

---

12. Eddy 1910, pp. 153-54.
13. Ibid., pp. 154-57.

popular belief in order to heal a single case of disease. ... Homoeopathy diminishes the drug, but the potency of the medicine increases as the drug disappears. Metaphysics, as taught in Christian Science, is the next stately step beyond homoeopathy. In metaphysics, matter disappears from the remedy entirely, and Mind takes its rightful and supreme place. Homoeopathy takes mental symptoms largely into consideration in its diagnosis of disease. Christian Science deals wholly with the mental cause in judging and destroying disease. It succeeds where homoeopathy fails, solely because its one recognized Principle of healing is Mind, and the whole force of the mental element is employed through the Science of Mind... Christian Science exterminates the drug, and rests on Mind alone as the curative Principle, acknowledging that the divine Mind has all power.[14]

So Eddy considered a quasi-continuum of progress as existing, with conventional medicine at one pole, homoeopathic medicine at some unspecified mid-point, and Christian Science at the opposite pole, representing the culmination of this development of understanding.

Observations and conclusions

Although twenty-first-century science and technology can sequence both the Spanish Influenza virus and the virus causing COVID-19 and the scanning electron microscope can even image individual virus particles, in Eddy's defence one has to consider the technological context in 1918-19. As a virus cannot replicate without the live cells of a host organism, attempting to culture and incubate one in a petri dish will not prove effective. Furthermore, as virtually all viruses are far smaller than the wavelength of light, they cannot be seen under any optical microscope – then or now – and those were the only microscopes available at that time. From the contemporary perspective of academic biology, therefore, one would have to postulate the existence of an invisible, seemingly nonreplicating organism as the hypothetical agent of contagion. Clearly, this does

---

14. Ibid., pp. 154-57.

not conform to the standards of objective science, and so Christian Science's objection to the medical consensus regarding Spanish Influenza is far more reasonable than it may first appear.

Regarding COVID-19, although Eddy would have been seen as a 'COVID denier', this would do her a disservice, despite being literally true. This is because her reasoning would not be based on paranoia, such as the belief that COVID-19 is a hoax designed to malignly manipulate the public, and would not be limited to just COVID-19, which is the case regarding 'true' COVID deniers. Although her position would be a far more extreme one, it is arguably more rational.

Regarding Eddy's view of homoeopathy as an intermediate step on the route to understanding the complete elimination of the role of matter, there is an analogy to be drawn with the present understanding of matter offered by nuclear physics, in which the structure of the atom is considered to be approximately one part per trillion matter by volume. Eddy's world model simply eliminates that last one-trillionth part.

Chapter 10

Penultimate Thoughts

The philosophical idealism underlying Mary Baker Eddy's system of thought has emerged in this book as a curious mixture of dazzling intellectual daring and, being very charitable, apparent occasional incoherency. Eddy comes across the 110-plus years since her death as a more wholehearted, more committed idealist thinker than many – perhaps all – famous philosophers in the field, and, somewhat counterintuitively, it is this unwavering approach which led to the possible problems regarding incoherency.

This final chapter will summarise her original contributions to the field, and also the ideas which she published before the academics who are known for them. For balance, the chapter also highlights the areas of her writing which remain problematic with regard to either their inconsistency within the system as a whole, or incoherency as it pertains to individual concepts.

The first original feature is that there are two components to Eddy's metaphysics: the aprioristic and the empirical. Her application of what is arguably scientific method (although one may dispute the choice of her experimental data, which ignores cases in which 'healings' have not occurred) creates what might be termed 'applied metaphysics'. The second observation is that there is considerable coherence in her thinking and a commitment to accept some highly counterintuitive consequences arising from it. This, I think, is particularly the hallmark of a philosopher. Thirdly, her claims and her method of arriving at them correspond to those of earlier and later academic philosophers. Fourthly, although her system of thought leads to objections that she may not be able to counter, this does not imply that no coherent philosophical argument is present. Many idealist philosophers can be refuted, and within general philosophy virtually all of the conclusions of the still-studied, highly respected Presocratic philosophers are no longer accepted without this affecting their status as philosophers.

The whole edifice of her thought (pun intended) relies on the nonexistence of matter. This is something that the British idealist John McTaggart concluded some decades later, with his most detailed argument for this position appearing in the second volume of *The Nature of Existence*[1].

The thorough analysis of Eddy's work provided by the previous chapters facilitates a parsimonious final description of her philosophical system. Although it offers a greater degree of self-consistency and coherency, albeit a very slightly artificial one, it is important to restate that consistency across the lifetime oeuvre of even first-rank academic philosophers is rarely present, if ever, and so judging Eddy's full set of texts on this basis would not constitute a fair approach unless it was also applied to other philosophers.

Eddy's philosophical system

The initial axioms are:

> Axiom 1. God is omniscient.
> Axiom 2. God is omnipotent.
> Axiom 3. God is omnipresent.
> Axiom 4. God is infinite.
> Axiom 5. God is (completely/infinitely) good.

Following from which Eddy constructs a system consisting of the following propositions:

> Proposition 1. God is infinite and unknowable, except by divine revelation and human conjecture.
> Proposition 2. God is Life, Truth, Love, Spirit, Principle, Mind and Good.
> Proposition 3. The hypothetical construct 'evil' is a 'delusion of material sense'.

---

1. McTaggart 1927, §§353-72.

Proposition 4. Nothing possesses reality or existence except divine Mind and His ideas.
Proposition 5. God fills all space, therefore all is Spirit.
Proposition 6. The triune nature of God consists of Life, Truth and Love.
Proposition 7. God is Father-Mother.
Proposition 8. The idea of Christ (not the human form) is eternal.
Proposition 9. The invisible Christ appears to the spiritual sense.
Proposition 10. Reality is spiritual, harmonious, immutable, immortal, divine [and] eternal.

This then leads immediately to the following corollaries:

Corollary 1. Illness, pain and death, as examples of the nonexistent human construct, 'evil', do not exist.
Corollary 2. As 'all is Spirit', and 'nothing possesses reality or existence except divine Mind and His ideas', as part of this reality we are therefore already perfect. Consequently, once a patient has been convinced of this their imaginary illness will disappear.
Corollary 3. If a patient experiences the disappearance of the signs and symptoms that resulted in them contacting a Christian Science practitioner, then this adds to the existing body of evidence of this type and increases the probability that the initial axioms and propositions are correct.

Remaining problems

At least three potentially serious problems have emerged from this analysis of Eddy's system of thought. Firstly, the variable degree of the isomorphism between 'spiritual reality' and its supposedly illusory physical counterpart (which gives rise to the specific problem regarding the accuracy of Eddy's perception of the Bible, upon which she placed considerable reliance); secondly the interpretation of infinity as 'everything', upon which Eddy's entire system relies; and thirdly, the paradox regarding the apparent error of being able

Penultimate Thoughts 163

to make errors, such as the error, as Eddy would see it, of believing in illness. The first problem could be considered as simply part of a human failing to understand 'divine Science' at this early stage, and the second problem has at least an avenue to a solution in the realm of transfinite numbers, but the third is more serious. If the determined attempt at a solution which this book represents is not accepted, then an alternative would be a prerequisite before accepting Eddy's philosophical system. Notwithstanding the above, whether this solution or another is accepted or not, Eddy's work is nevertheless highly original, radically idealist philosophy. The case is proven for Eddy being a philosopher, but the jury still is out regarding to what degree she was right.

An alternative interpretation

Using the same approach as Eddy, but interpreting the evidence of our senses at face value, could one conclude the exact opposite to her? It would be as follows:

1. Simply pain, illness and death exist.
2. The perception of freedom from pain is an illusion.
3. The perception of freedom from illness is an illusion.
4. Only the devil exists, who is entirely evil and, being unlimited, occupies all space; everything is therefore evil, necessarily including humans. There is therefore no 'good', and only evil exists.
5. Simply the physical universe exists; metaphysical and spiritual entities are fictional.
6. The devil, given the point immediately above, physically exists.

What evidence would support this set of concepts? It could be as follows:

1. Prayer does not work on the majority of occasions, and even when it appears to, this could be illusory.
2. Dreadful suffering is sometimes experienced by the completely innocent, such as very young children.

3. The majority of deaths in wartime are civilians.
4. For much of the world's population, war is the modal state, even to the point that many young people, both children and young adults, have never experienced peace time.
5. In many developing countries, illnesses which would be easily treatable in richer nations can prove fatal due to either the lack of the necessary drugs or the unavailability of medical equipment. Even in wealthier jurisdictions, if healthcare is not funded by the state, the above situation can also be the frequent experience of the poor.

Curiously, this seemingly self-consistent alternative immediately faces a fundamental difficulty. If only physical entities – matter and energy – exist, what is consciousness, or the experience of pain? They appear to be neither matter nor energy in themselves, despite being caused by and modifiable by matter and energy. 'Evil', too, seems similarly problematic.

Still greater radicalism

Although Eddy's philosophy appears to be an example of the limiting case of radical idealism, this could of course be a mistake. It would be interesting intellectual puzzle to attempt to construct a still more extreme system, and although the fact that her system is based on the zealous rejection of all things material might seem to imply that this would be an impossible task, there is a precedent offered in the work of the previously mentioned Christian Scientist, Emma Curtiss Hopkins, who developed her own form of metaphysical healing following her dismissal by Eddy. She stated that: 'There are other things besides sickness and sin which can be denied out of existence by our word. If we are in poverty, trouble, anxiety, name the state or condition and *deny it*' [my italics][2]. Hopkins agreed with Eddy regarding the universe being Spirit, so if the above applies to all abstract concepts and propositions, then nothing would appear to be safe from denial, even including the concept of denial itself!

---

2. Hopkins 1923, p. 173.

Suggestions for further research

Epistemologically, Christian Science is a curious combination of both fideism and correspondent truth. Fideism in that Eddy asserts the existence of spiritual sense, along with her acceptance of the complete accuracy of the Bible, seemingly on the basis of faith; correspondent truth, however, Eddy relies upon with regard to her healings as 'proof' of the correctness of her system of thought. Although this could be characterised as an inconsistency of her approach, another reading could be that each form of truth is appropriate within the two magisteria straddled by Christian Science – the metaphysical and the empirical. Exploring what might be termed 'fideist correspondence', or 'correspondent fideism', would be interesting in itself, as would seeking other examples (if they exist) of its occurrence in existing work.

Finally

This book ends by giving Eddy the last word. As an example of her sheer daring, the interpretation she provides for the Lord's Prayer seems unequalled. Given the limitations imposed by the necessity to communicate ideas in 'natural' language, it is Eddy at her very best; truly 'The dream and the dreamer are one'[3].

> Our Father, which art in heaven.
> *Our Father-Mother God, all-harmonious.*
> Hallowed be thy name.
> *Adorable One.*
> Thy kingdom come.
> *Thy kingdom is come; Thou art ever-present.*
> Thy will be done on earth, as it is in heaven.
> *Enable us to know, – as in heaven, so on earth, – God is omnipotent, supreme.*
> Give us this day our daily bread;
> *Give us grace for to-day; feed the famished affections;*
> And forgive us our debts, as we forgive our debtors.
> *And Love is reflected in love;*

---

3. Eddy 1910, p. 530.

> And lead us not into temptation, but deliver us from evil;
> *And God leadeth us not into temptation, but deliver us from sin, disease, and death.*
> For Thine is the kingdom, and the power, and the glory, forever.
> *For God is infinite, all-power, all Life, Truth, Love, over all, and All.*[4]

And that is precisely what Christian Science is about. If we accept Eddy's system, then the naïve, physicalist world view is a great myth. Love stories are real, and we are in one, but the true surprise is that everything which exists is just one thing, and that, in the fullest sense, is Love.

---

4. Eddy 1910, pp. 16-17.

Bibliography

Armstrong, David M. (1963), 'Is Introspection Incorrigible?', *Philosophical Review* 72, no. 3, pp. 417-32
Barth, Karl (1936) *Church Dogmatics I.1*, Edinburgh: T. & T. Clark.
Barth, Karl (1956) *Church Dogmatics I.2*, Edinburgh: T. & T. Clark.
Barth, Karl (1956) *Church Dogmatics IV.1*, Edinburgh: T. & T. Clark.
Barth, Karl (1957) *Church Dogmatics II.1*, Edinburgh: T. & T. Clark.
Barth, Karl (1957) *Church Dogmatics II.2*, Edinburgh: T. & T. Clark.
Barth, Karl (1958) *Church Dogmatics III.1*, Edinburgh: T. & T. Clark.
Barth, Karl (1958) *Church Dogmatics IV.2*, Edinburgh: T. & T. Clark.
Barth, Karl (1960) *Church Dogmatics III.2*, Edinburgh: T. & T. Clark.
Barth, Karl (1960) *Church Dogmatics III.3*, Edinburgh: T. & T. Clark.
Barth, Karl (1961) *Church Dogmatics IV.3.1*, Edinburgh: T. & T. Clark.
Barth, Karl (1961) *Church Dogmatics IV.3.2*, Edinburgh: T. & T. Clark.
Barth, Karl (1969) *Church Dogmatics IV.4*, Edinburgh: T. & T. Clark.
Bates, Ernest S. and John V. Dittemore (1932), *Mary Baker Eddy: The Truth and the Tradition* (New York: A.A. Knopf)
Beasley, Norman (1957), *The Continuing Spirit* (London: Allen and Unwin)
Bergson, Gerald (2001) *The Christian Science Holocaust* (Danbury: The New England Skeptical Society)
Berkeley, George (1948-1957) *The Works of George Berkeley, Bishop of Cloyne*. Edited by A. A. Luce and T. E. Jessop. 9 volumes. (London: Thomas Nelson and Sons)
Blavatsky, Helena (1907), *Some of the Errors of Christian Science* (Point Loma: Aryan Theosophical Press)
Braden, Charles S. (1967), [Review of *Mary Baker Eddy, the Years of Discovery*, by R. Peel], *Journal for the Scientific Study of Religion* 6, no. 2, pp. 294-96
Bradley, Francis H. (1876), *Ethical Studies* (London: Henry S. King and Co.)
Bradley, Francis H. (1893), *Appearance and Reality* (London: S. Sonnenschein; New York: Macmillan)

Braude, Ann (2007) *Sisters and Saints: Women and American Religion*, (New York: Oxford University Press)

Brock, R. Lillian, Agnes F. Chalmers and Edward W. Dickey (1922), *Christian Science War Time Activities* (Boston: Christian Science Publishing Society)

Buckley, James H. (1901), 'The Absurd Paradox of Christian Science', *The North American Review* 173, no. 536, pp. 22-34

Burnet, John (1920) *Early Greek Philosophy* (London and Edinburgh: A. and C. Black) 3rd edition

Butler, Judith (1999 [1990]), *Gender Trouble: Feminism and the Subversion of Identity* (New York: Routledge)

Cantor, Georg (1895) 'Beiträge zur Begründung der transfiniten Mengenlehre (1)' *Mathematische Annalen*. 46 (4): 481–512

Clark, Ronald (2007) *Einstein: The Life and Times* (New York: William Morrow)

Clemens, Clara (1956), *Awake to a Perfect Day: My Experiences with Christian Science* (New York: The Citadel Press)

Cunningham, Raymond J (Abridger) (1975) *Cotton Mather Magnalia Christi Americana; Or, the Ecclesiastical History of New England*, (New York: Ungar Publishing Company)

Dakin, Edwin F. (1929) *Mrs. Eddy, the biography of a virginal mind* : Charles Scribner

[Dickson, Carol E. (1998). "Eddy, Mary Baker 1821–1910". In Amico, Eleanor B. (ed.). *Reader's guide to women's studies*. (Chicago and London: Fitzroy)

Dearborn, R. J. (2000), 'Genomics Happens', *Science* 289, no. 5484, pp. 1488-89

Dresser, Horatio W. (1921), *The Quimby Manuscript, Showing the Discovery of Spiritual Healing and the Origin of Christian Science* (New York: Thomas Y. Cromwell)

Dyck, Cornelius J. (1968), "Reviewed Work(s): Christian Science: Its Encounter with American Culture by Robert Peel". *Review of Religious Research*. **9** *(2): 123–124*

Eddy, Mary Baker (1883), *People's Idea of God* (Boston: Christian Science Publishing Society)

Eddy, Mary Baker (1887a), *No and Yes* (Boston: Christian Science Publishing Society)

Eddy, Mary Baker (1887b), *Rudimental Divine Science* (Boston: Christian Science Publishing Society)

Eddy, Mary Baker (1888), *Unity of Good* (Boston: Christian Science Publishing Society)

Eddy, Mary Baker (1891), *Retrospection and Introspection* (Boston: Christian Science Publishing Society)

Eddy, Mary Baker (1893), *Christ and Christmas* (Boston: Christian Science Publishing Society)
Eddy, Mary Baker (1895), *Manual of the Mother Church* (Boston: Christian Science Publishing Society)
Eddy, Mary Baker (1895) *Pulpit and Press* (Boston: Christian Science Publishing Society)
Eddy, Mary Baker (1897), *Miscellaneous Writings 1883-1896* (Boston: Christian Science Publishing Society)
Eddy, Mary Baker (1898), *Christian Science versus Pantheism* (Boston: Christian Science Publishing Society)
Eddy, Mary Baker (1910 [1875]), *Science and Health with Key to the Scriptures* (Boston: Christian Science Publishing Society)
Eddy, Mary Baker (1913), *The First Church of Christ, Scientist, and Miscellany* (Boston: Christian Science Publishing Society)
Edwards, Jonathan (1836 [1739]) *A History of the Work of Redemption*, (London: Religious Tract Society)
Einstein, Albert (1920) *Relativity: The Special and General Theory*, trans. Robert W. Lawson, (New York: Henry Holt and Company)
Emerson, Ralph W. (1836)*Nature*, (Boston: James Munroe and Co.)
Enfield, William (1837)] *The History of Philosophy From the Earliest Periods*, (London: Thomas Tegg and Son). The fourth edition of a translation of Johann Jakob Bruckner's *Historia Critica Philosphiae*, first published in six volumes in 1742-67
Evans, Warren F. (1869), *The Mental-Cure, Illustrating the Influence of the Mind on the Body, Both in Health and Disease, and the Psychological Method of Treatment* (Boston: Carter)
Farnsworth, Edward C. (1909), *The Sophistries of Christian Science* (Portland: Smith & Sale)
Ferreirós, José (2007). *Labyrinth of Thought: A History of Set Theory and Its Role in Mathematical Thought.* (Basel, Switzerland: Birkhäuser)
Fichte, Johann G. (1987 [1800]), *The Vocation of Man*, trans. P. Preuss (Indianapolis: Hackett)
Findlay, James (1967*)* "Mary Baker Eddy: The Years of Discovery. By Robert Peel" (book review) *Journal of American History*, Volume 53, Issue 4, March 1967, pp. 834–836,
[Fox, Matthew (1996) *The Making of a Post-Denominational Priest* (North Atlantic Books)]
Gill, Gillian (1998), *Mary Baker Eddy* (Boston, Mass.: Da Capo Press)
Gilmore, Davye M. (1935), 'Of This I Am Sure', *The Christian Science Journal* 53, no. 8, November
Gotshalk, Dilman W. (1930), 'McTaggart on Time', *Mind* 39, no. 153, pp. 26-42

Gottschalk, Stephen (1973), *The Emergence of Christian Science in American Religious Life* (Berkeley: University of California Press)
Gottschalk, Stephen (1987), *The Christian Science Monitor*, 5 August 1987.
Gottschalk, Stephen (2006), *Rolling Away the Stone: Mary Baker Eddy's Challenge to Materialism* (Bloomington: Indiana University Press)
Grodzins, Dean (2002) *American Heretic: Theodore Parker and Transcendentalism* (Chapel Hill and London: University of North Carolina Press)
Gura, Philip (2007) 'The Transcendentalist Commotion' *New England Review* Vol. 28 No. 3 pp. 50-78.
Hammond, Edward H. (1899), 'Christian Science: What It Is and What It Does', *The Christian Science Journal* 17, no. 7, p. 464
Hegel, Georg W.F. (1977 [1807]), *Phenomenology of Spirit*, trans. Arnold V. Miller (Oxford: Clarendon Press)
Heisenberg, Werner (1927) "Ueber den anschaulichen Inhalt der quantentheoretischen Kinematik and Mechanik", *Zeitschrift für Physik*, 43: 172–198. For an English translation see Wheeler and Zurek (1983) pp. 62–84.
Hopkins, Emma Curtis (1923) *High Mysticism*, (Cornwall Bridge: High Watch Fellowship)
Henry, Matthew (1960 [1708]) *Matthew Henry's Commentary on the Whole Bible in One Volume*, Church, Leslie F. (editor), London: Marshall, Morgan and Scott.
Hopkins, Emma Curtiss (1888), *First Lessons in Christian Science* (Chicago: Purdy)
Hunter, Rodney (ed.) (1990), *Dictionary of Pastoral Care and Counselling* (Nashville: Abingdon), pp. 152-54
Ingle. H. Larry (1996) *First Among Friends: George Fox & the Creation of Quakerism* Oxford: Oxford University Press
Ingthorsson, Rögnvaldur D. (1998), 'McTaggart and the Unreality of Time', *Axiomathes* 9, no. 3, pp. 287-306
Ingthorsson, Rögnvaldur D. (2001), 'Temporal Parity and the Problem of Change', *SATS – Nordic Journal of Philosophy* 2, no. 2, pp. 60-79
Ingthorsson, Rögnvaldur D. (2016), *McTaggart's Paradox* (New York: Routledge)
Isaacson, Walter (2008) *Einstein: His Life and Universe* (London: Simon and Schuster)
Jolley, Nicholas (1990) *The light of the soul: theories of ideas in Leibniz, Malebranche, and Descartes*, (New York: Oxford University Press)
Keyston, David, L. (1996) *The Healer: The Healing Work of Mary Baker Eddy* Van Nuys, (California: Aequus Institute Publications)
Kirk, Geoffrey, Raven, John and Schofield, Malcolm (1983) *The Presocratic Philosophers*, (London: Cambridge University Press)

Knapp, Bliss. (1991) *The Destiny of The Mother Church*. Christian Science Publishing Society
Kuo, Zing-Yang (1922), 'How Are Our Instincts Acquired?', *Psychological Review* 29, no. 5, pp. 344-65
Lewis, Clive S. (1952), *Mere Christianity* (London: Collins)
Lipton, Bruce H. (2005), *The Biology of Belief* (Llandeilo: Cygnus Books.)
MacIntosh, Douglas Clyde (1919), *Theology as an Empirical Science* (Milton Keynes: Bibliolife)
Malebranche, Nicolas (1958-84), *Œuvres complètes de Malebranche* (20 volumes), ed. A. Robinet (Paris: J. Vrin)
Malebranche, Nicolas (1980a), *Dialogues on Metaphysics*, trans. W. Doney (New York: Abaris Books)
Malebranche, Nicolas (1980b), *Nature of God*, trans. D.A. Iorio (Washington, DC: Catholic University Press)
Malebranche, Nicolas (1980c), *The Search after Truth*, trans. T.M. Lennon and P.J. Olscamp (Columbus: Ohio State University Press)
Malebranche, Nicolas (1993), *Treatise on Ethics*, trans. C. Walton (Dordrecht: Kluwer)
Malebranche, Nicolas (1997), *Dialogues on Metaphysics and on Religion*, trans. N. Jolley and D. Scott (Cambridge: Cambridge University Press)
Martin, Walter R. (1955) *The Christian Science Myth*, (Grand Rapids: Zondervan)
Marty, Martin E. (1978), 'Religious Books', *The New York Times Book Review*, 12 March 1978, p. 41
McCorkle, Rev. W.P. (1899), *Christian Science, or the False Christ of 1866* (Richmond: Whittet and Shepperson)
McCracken, Charles (1983) 'Malebranche and British Philosophy' *Revue Philosophique de la France Et de l'Etranger* 173 (4):467-468.
McTaggart, John M.E. (1908), 'The Unreality of Time', *Mind* 17, no. 68, pp. 457-73
McTaggart, John M.E. (1921, 1927), *The Nature of Existence* (2 vols) (London: Cambridge University Press)
Mesmer, Franz (1779), *Memoire sur la decourverte du magnetisme animal* (Geneva and Paris: Didot le jeune), trans. (1948) Gilbert Frankau, *Mesmerism by Doctor Mesmer* (London: MacDonald) [English translation of the original]
Messenger, Frank (1856) *The Time of the End*, (Boston: J.P Jewett and Company)
Milmine, Georgine (1909) *The Life of Mary Baker G. Eddy and the History of Christian Science*, (London: Hodder and Stoughton)
Moore, G.E. (1903), 'The Refutation of Idealism', *Mind* 12, no. 4, pp. 433-53

Nadler, Steven M. (1992) *Malebranche and ideas*, (New York: Oxford University Press)
Nadler, Steven M. (ed.) (2000) *The Cambridge companion to Malebranche*, (New York: Cambridge University Press)
Nadler, Steven (2024), 'Baruch Spinoza', in *The Stanford Encyclopedia of Philosophy* (Spring 2024 edition), ed. Edward N. Zalta and Uri Nodelman, https://plato.stanford.edu/archives/spr2024/entries/spinoza/
Nenneman, Richard A. (1997), *Persistent Pilgrim: The Life of Mary Baker Eddy* (Etna: Nebbadoon Press)
Nikkel, David H. (1995), *Panentheism in Hartshorne and Tillich: A Creative Synthesis* (New York: Peter Lang)
'Novalis' (2007 [1798, 1799]), *Notes for a Romantic Encyclopaedia*, ed. and trans. David W. Wood (Albany: State University of New York Press)
Orcutt, William D. (1950), *Mary Baker Eddy and Her Books* (Boston: Christian Science Publishing Society)
Paine, Albert Bigelow (1912) *Mark Twain A Biography*, (New York: Harpers and Brothers Publishers)
Patterson, Charles Brook (1905), *What the New Thought Stands For* (New York: Alliance)
Peel, Robert (1958). *Christian Science: Its Encounter with American Culture*, (New York: Henry Holt and Company)
Peel, Robert (1966) *Mary Baker Eddy: The Years of Discovery*. (New York: Holt, Rinehart and Winston)
Peel, Robert (1971). *Mary Baker Eddy: The Years of Trial*. (New York: Holt, Rinehart and Winston)
Peel, Robert (1977). *Mary Baker Eddy: The Years of Authority*. (New York: Holt, Rinehart and Winston)
Peel, Robert (1969), 'The Christian Science Practitioner', *Journal of Pastoral Counselling* 4, no. 1, Spring 1969, pp. 39-42
Peel, Robert (1987), *Spiritual Healing in a Scientific Age* (San Francisco: Harper & Row)
Peppers-Bates, Susan (2009) *Nicolas Malebranche: Freedom in an Occasionalist World* (London and New York: Continuum)
Polkinghorne, John (1988), *Science and Creation* (London: SPCK)
Putnam, Hilary (2012), 'How to be a Sophisticated Naive Realist' in *Philosophy in an Age of Science*, ed. Mario de Caro and David Macarthur (Cambridge: Harvard University Press), pp. 624-39
Pyle, Andrew (2003) *Malebranche* (New York: Routledge)
Quimby, Phineas Parkhurst: despite his importance to the subject, Quimby did not publish in his lifetime; see Dresser 1921 for his work
Radner, Daisie (1978) *Malebranche: a study of a Cartesian system* (Assen: Van Gorcum)
Raff, Charles (1966), 'Introspection and Incorrigibility', *Philosophy and Phenomenological Research* 80, pp. 595-637

Rosenau, Milton J. (1919), 'Experiments to Determine Mode of Spread of Influenza', *Journal of the American Medical Association* 73, no. 5, p. 313

Rovelli, Carlo (2015), 'Aristotle's Physics: A Physicist's Look', *Journal of the American Philosophical Association* 1, no. 1, pp. 23-40

Rucker, Rudy (1982), *Infinity and the Mind: The Science and Philosophy of the Infinite* (Princeton: Princeton University Press)

Russell, Bertrand (1996 [1903]). *The Principles of Mathematics*. 2d. ed. Reprint, (New York: W. W. Norton & Company)

Satter, Beryl (1999), *Each Mind a Kingdom: American Women, Sexual Purity, and the New Thought Movement, 1875-1920* (Berkeley: University of California Press)

Schelling, Friedrich W.J. (1978 [1800]), *System of Transcendental Idealism*, trans. P. Heath, intr. M. Vater (Charlottesville: University Press of Virginia)

Schmaltz, Tad M. (1996) *Malebranche's theory of the soul: a Cartesian interpretation* (New York: Oxford University Press)

Schopenhauer, Arthur (1851), *Parerga and Paralipomena* (Berlin: Hayn)

Sheldon, Georgina (1904), *Katherine's Sheaves* (New York: The Federal Book Club)

Sheldrake, Philip (2018) *Julian of Norwich: In God's Sight* Hoboken, (New Jersey: Wiley Blackwell)

Shepherd, Odell (ed.) (1938), *The Journals of Bronson Alcott* (Boston: Little, Brown)

Siewers, Alfred K (2019). *How Christian Science Became a Dying Religion*. TheFederalist.com, April 11

Smith, Nicholas J.J. (2011), 'Inconsistency in the A-Theory', *Philosophical Studies* 156, no. 2, pp. 231-47

Spinoza, Baruch (1887 [1677]) *The Chief Works of Benedict de Spinoza*. Two Vols. (trans R.H.M. Elwes) (London: George Bell and Sons)

Stark, Rodney (1998), 'The Rise and Fall of Christian Science', *Journal of Contemporary Religion* 13, no. 2, pp. 189-214

Steiger, Henry W. (1946), 'A Philosophical Investigation of the Doctrine of Christian Science' (PhD dissertation, Boston University)

Steiger, Henry W. (1948), *Christian Science and Philosophy* (New York: Philosophical Library)

Thomas, Emily (2018), *Early Modern Women on Metaphysics* (Cambridge: Cambridge University Press)

Thomas, Wendell (1930) *Hinduism Invades America* (New York: The Beacon Press)

Torrance, Thomas F. (1969), *Theological Science* (London: Oxford University Press)

Twain, Mark (1907), *Christian Science* (New York and London: Harper Brothers)

Twain, Mark (1916), *No. 44, The Mysterious Stranger* (New York: Harper Brothers)

Voorhees, Amy B. (2021), *A New Christian Identity: Christian Science Origins and Experience in American Culture* (Chapel Hill: University of North Carolina Press)

Walton, Craig (1972) *De la Recherche du Bien A Study of Malebranche's Science of Ethics* (The Hague: Martinus Nijhoff)

Watson, John B. (1913), 'Psychology as the Behaviorist Views It', *Psychological Review* 20, no. 2, pp. 158-77

Wheeler, J.A. and W.H. Zurek (eds), (1983), *Quantum Theory and Measurement*, (Princeton, NJ: Princeton University Press)

Wilbur, Sibyl (1913), *The Life of Mary Baker Eddy*, 4th edition (Boston: Christian Science Publishing Society)

Wilcox, Martha (1941), 'Association Address', Healing Unlimited Association

Wolcott, Peter C. (1896), *What is Christian Science*? (New York: Revell)

Glossary

In addition to a subset of individual terms reproduced as defined (or redefined) by Eddy in Chapter 17 of *Science and Health*[1], this glossary includes the present author's explanation of words and phrases which also could otherwise lead to misunderstandings. Definitions of the latter form all begin with the phrase 'In Christian Science', so as to distinguish them from those selected from Eddy's own glossary.

ADAM. Error; a falsity; the belief in 'original sin,' sickness, and death; evil; the opposite of good, – of God and His creation; a curse; a belief in intelligent matter, finiteness, and mortality; 'dust to dust;' red sandstone; nothingness; the first god of mythology; not God's man, who represents the one God and is His own image and likeness; the opposite of Spirit and His creations; that which is not the image and likeness of good, but a material belief, opposed to the one Mind, or Spirit; a so-called finite mind, producing other minds, thus making 'gods many and lords many' (I Corinthians viii. 5); a product of nothing as the mimicry of something; an unreality as opposed to the great reality of spiritual existence and creation; a so-called man, whose origin, substance, and mind are found to be the antipode of God, or Spirit; an inverted image of Spirit; the image and likeness of what God has not created, namely, matter, sin, sickness, and death; the opposer of Truth, termed error; Life's counterfeit, which ultimates in death; the opposite of Love, called hate; the usurper of Spirit's creation, called self-creative matter; immortality's opposite, mortality; that of which wisdom saith, 'Thou shalt surely die.'

---

1. Eddy 1910, pp. 579 ff.

The name Adam represents the false supposition that Life is not eternal, but has beginning and end; that the infinite enters the finite, that intelligence passes into non-intelligence, and that Soul dwells in material sense; that immortal Mind results in matter, and matter in mortal mind; that the one God and creator entered what He created, and then disappeared in the atheism of matter.

ANGELS. God's thoughts passing to man; spiritual intuitions, pure and perfect; the inspiration of goodness, purity, and immortality, counteracting all evil, sensuality, and mortality.

ARK. Safety; the idea, or reflection, of Truth, proved to be as immortal as its Principle; the understanding of Spirit, destroying belief in matter.

God and man coexistent and eternal; Science showing that the spiritual realities of all things are created by Him and exist forever. The ark indicates temptation overcome and followed by exaltation.

ATONEMENT. Not Christ's sacrifice paying the 'debt' of humanity, but 'at-one-ment'. 'The atonement of Christ reconciles man to God, not God to man; for the divine Principle of Christ is God, and how can God propitiate Himself?' (Eddy 1910, p. 18). Additionally, 'Jesus aided in reconciling man to God by giving man a truer sense of Love, the divine Principle of Jesus' teachings, and this truer sense of Love redeems man from the law of matter, sin, and death by the law of Spirit, – the law of divine Love' (ibid.).

BABEL. Self-destroying error; a kingdom divided against itself, which cannot stand; material knowledge.

The higher false knowledge builds on the basis of evidence obtained from the five corporeal senses, the more confusion ensues, and the more certain is the downfall of its structure.

BENJAMIN (Jacob's son). A physical belief as to life, substance, and mind; human knowledge, or so-called mortal mind, devoted to matter; pride; envy; fame; illusion; a false belief; error masquerading as the possessor of life, strength, animation, and power to act.

Renewal of affections; self-offering; an improved state of mortal mind; the introduction of a more spiritual origin; a gleam of the infinite idea of the infinite Principle; a spiritual type; that which comforts, consoles, and supports.

Glossary

BLASPHEMY. In Christian Science, the idea that God would create an imperfect universe is blasphemous, as it would imply that God was not omnipotent and not perfect.

BRIDE. Purity and innocence, conceiving man in the idea of God; a sense of Soul, which has spiritual bliss and enjoys but cannot suffer.

BRIDEGROOM. Spiritual understanding; the pure consciousness that God, the divine Principle, creates man as His own spiritual idea, and that God is the only creative power.

CANAAN (the son of Ham). A sensuous belief; the testimony of what is termed material sense; the error which would make man mortal and would make mortal mind a slave to the body.

CHILDREN. The spiritual thoughts and representatives of Life, Truth, and Love. Sensual and mortal beliefs; counterfeits of creation, whose better originals are God's thoughts, not in embryo, but in maturity; material suppositions of life, substance, and intelligence, opposed to the Science of being.

CHILDREN OF ISRAEL. The representatives of Soul, not corporeal sense; the offspring of Spirit, who, having wrestled with error, sin, and sense, are governed by divine Science; some of the ideas of God beheld as men, casting out error and healing the sick; Christ's offspring.

CHRIST. The divine manifestation of God, which comes to the flesh to destroy incarnate error.

CHURCH. The structure of Truth and Love; whatever rests upon and proceeds from divine Principle.

The Church is that institution, which affords proof of its utility and is found elevating the race, rousing the dormant understanding from material beliefs to the apprehension of spiritual ideas and the demonstration of divine Science, thereby casting out devils, or error, and healing the sick.

CREATION. In Christian Science, God and the divine thoughts of God are the entirety of existence and therefore all of creation.

DAN (Jacob's son). Animal magnetism; so-called mortal mind controlling mortal mind; error, working out the designs of error; one belief preying upon another.

DAY. The irradiance of Life; light, the spiritual idea of Truth and Love.

'And the evening and the morning were the first day.' (Genesis i. 5.) The objects of time and sense disappear in the illumination of spiritual understanding, and Mind measures time according to the good that is unfolded. This unfolding is God's day, and 'there shall be no night there.'

DEATH. An illusion, the lie of life in matter; the unreal and untrue; the opposite of Life.

Matter has no life, hence it has no real existence. Mind is immortal. The flesh, warring against Spirit; that which frets itself free from one belief only to be fettered by another, until every belief of life where Life is not yields to eternal Life. Any material evidence of death is false, for it contradicts the spiritual facts of being.

DEVIL. Evil; a lie; error; neither corporeality nor mind; the opposite of Truth; a belief in sin, sickness, and death; animal magnetism or hypnotism; the lust of the flesh, which saith: 'I am life and intelligence in matter. There is more than one mind, for I am mind, – a wicked mind, self-made or created by a tribal god and put into the opposite of mind, termed matter, thence to reproduce a mortal universe, including man, not after the image and likeness of Spirit, but after its own image.'

DOVE. A symbol of divine Science; purity and peace; hope and faith.

DUST. Nothingness; the absence of substance, life, or intelligence.

EARS. Not organs of the so-called corporeal senses, but spiritual understanding.

Jesus said, referring to spiritual perception, 'Having ears, hear ye not?' (Mark viii. 18.)

EVE. A beginning; mortality; that which does not last forever; a finite belief concerning life, substance, and intelligence in matter; error; the belief that the human race originated materially instead of spiritually, – that man started first from dust, second from a rib, and third from an egg.

EVIL. In Christian Science, evil in the conventionally understood meaning does not exist, being simply a false belief; Eddy's preferred term for the category of false beliefs is 'error'.

Glossary

EYES. Spiritual discernment, – not material but mental.

Jesus said, thinking of the outward vision, 'Having eyes, see ye not?' (Mark viii. 18.)

FIRMAMENT. Spiritual understanding; the scientific line of demarcation between Truth and error, between Spirit and so-called matter.

FLESH. An error of physical belief; a supposition that life, substance, and intelligence are in matter; an illusion; a belief that matter has sensation.

GETHSEMANE. Patient woe; the human yielding to the divine; love meeting no response, but still remaining love.

GHOST. An illusion; a belief that mind is outlined and limited; a supposition that spirit is finite.

GOD. The great I AM; the all-knowing, all-seeing, all-acting, all-wise, all-loving, and eternal; Principle; Mind; Soul; Spirit; Life; Truth; Love; all substance; intelligence.

GODS. Mythology; a belief that life, substance, and intelligence are both mental and material; a supposition of sentient physicality; the belief that infinite Mind is in finite forms; the various theories that hold mind to be a material sense, existing in brain, nerve, matter; supposititious minds, or souls, going in and out of matter, erring and mortal; the serpents of error, which say, 'Ye shall be as gods.'

God is one God, infinite and perfect, and cannot become finite and imperfect.

HAM (Noah's son). Corporeal belief; sensuality; slavery; tyranny.

HEAVEN. Harmony; the reign of Spirit; government by divine Principle; spirituality; bliss; the atmosphere of Soul.

HELL. Mortal belief; error; lust; remorse; hatred; revenge; sin; sickness; death; suffering and self-destruction, self-imposed agony; effects of sin; that which 'worketh abomination or maketh a lie.'

HIDDEKEL (river). Divine Science understood and acknowledged.

HOLY GHOST. Divine Science; the development of eternal Life, Truth, and Love.

I, or EGO. Divine Principle; Spirit; Soul; incorporeal, unerring, immortal, and eternal Mind.

There is but one I, or Us, but one divine Principle, or Mind, governing all existence; man and woman unchanged forever in their individual characters, even as numbers which never blend with each other, though they are governed by one Principle. All the objects of God's creation reflect one Mind, and whatever reflects not this one Mind, is false and erroneous, even the belief that life, substance, and intelligence are both mental and material.

I AM. God; incorporeal and eternal Mind; divine Principle; the only Ego.

JAPHET (Noah's son). A type of spiritual peace, flowing from the understanding that God is the divine Principle of all existence, and that man is His idea, the child of His care.

JERUSALEM. Mortal belief and knowledge obtained from the five corporeal senses; the pride of power and the power of pride; sensuality; envy; oppression; tyranny. Home, heaven.

JESUS. The highest human corporeal concept of the divine idea, rebuking and destroying error and bringing to light man's immortality.

JOSEPH. A corporeal mortal; a higher sense of Truth rebuking mortal belief, or error, and showing the immortality and supremacy of Truth; pure affection blessing its enemies.

JUDAH. A corporeal material belief progressing and disappearing; the spiritual understanding of God and man appearing.

KINGDOM OF HEAVEN. The rein of harmony in divine Science; the realm of unerring, eternal, and omnipotent Mind; the atmosphere of Spirit, where Soul is supreme.

KNOWLEDGE. Evidence obtained from the five corporeal senses; mortality; beliefs and opinions; human theories, doctrines, hypotheses; that which is not divine and is the origin of sin, sickness, and death; the opposite of spiritual Truth and understanding.

LAMB OF GOD. The spiritual idea of Love; self-immolation; innocence and purity; sacrifice.

MAN. The compound idea of infinite Spirit; the spiritual image and likeness of God; the full representation of Mind.

MATTER. Mythology; mortality; another name for mortal mind; illusion; intelligence, substance, and life in non-intelligence and mortality; life resulting in death, and death in life; sensation in the sensationless; mind originating in matter; the opposite of Truth; the opposite of Spirit; the opposite of God; that of which immortal Mind takes no cognizance; that which mortal mind sees, feels, hears, tastes, and smells only in belief.

MIND. The only I, or Us; the only Spirit, Soul, divine Principle, substance, Life, Truth, Love; the one God; not that which is *in* man, but the divine Principle, or God, of whom man is the full and perfect expression; Deity, which outlines but is not outlined.

MIRACLE. That which is divinely natural, but must be learned humanly; a phenomenon of Science.

MORNING. Light; symbol of Truth; revelation and progress.

MORTAL MIND. Nothing claiming to be something, for Mind is immortal; mythology; error creating other errors; a suppositional material sense, alias the belief that sensation is in matter, which is sensationless; a belief that life, substance, and intelligence are in and of matter; the opposite of Spirit, and therefore the opposite of God, or good; the belief that life has a beginning and therefore an end; the belief that man is the offspring of mortals; the belief that there can be more than one creator; idolatry; the subjective states of error; material senses; that which neither exists in Science nor can be recognized by the spiritual sense; sin; sickness; death.

MOSES. A corporeal mortal; moral courage; a type of moral law and the demonstration thereof; the proof that, without the gospel, – the union of justice and affection, – there is something spiritually lacking, since justice demands penalties under the law.

MOTHER. God; divine and eternal Principle; Life, Truth, and Love.

NEW JERUSALEM. Divine Science; the spiritual facts and harmony of the universe; the kingdom of heaven, or reign of harmony.

NIGHT. Darkness; doubt; fear.

NOAH. A corporeal mortal; knowledge of the nothingness of material things and of the immortality of all that is spiritual.

PHARISEE. Corporeal and sensuous belief; self-righteousness; vanity; hypocrisy.

PROPHET. A spiritual seer; disappearance of material sense before the conscious facts of spiritual Truth.

RIVER. Channel of thought.

When smooth and unobstructed, it typifies the course of Truth; but muddy, foaming, and dashing, it is a type of error.

SERPENT (*ophis*, in Greek; *nacash*, in Hebrew). Subtlety; a lie; the opposite of Truth, named error; the first statement of mythology and idolatry; the belief in more than one God; animal magnetism; the first lie of limitation; finity; the first claim that there is an opposite of Spirit, or good, termed matter, or evil; the first delusion that error exists as fact; the first claim that sin, sickness, and death are the realities of life. The first audible claim that God was not omnipotent and that there was another power, named *evil*, which was as real and eternal as God, good.

SHEM (Noah's son). A corporeal mortal; kindly affection; love rebuking error; reproof of sensualism.

SPIRIT. Divine substance; Mind; divine Principle; all that is good; God; that only which is perfect, everlasting, omnipresent, omnipotent, infinite.

SUN. The symbol of Soul governing man, – of Truth, Life, and Love.

SWORD. The idea of Truth; justice. Revenge; anger.

THUMMIM. Perfection; the eternal demand of divine Science.

The Urim and Thummim, which were to be on Aaron's breast when he went before Jehovah, were holiness and purification of thought and deed, which alone can fit us for the office of spiritual teaching.

UNCLEANLINESS. Impure thoughts; error; sin; dirt.

UNKNOWN. That which spiritual sense alone comprehends, and which is unknown to the material senses.

Paganism and agnosticism may define Deity as 'the great unknowable;' but Christian Science brings God much nearer to man, and makes Him better known as the All-in-all, forever near.

Paul saw in Athens an altar dedicated 'to the unknown God.' Referring to it, he said to the Athenians: 'Whom therefore ye ignorantly worship, Him declare I unto you.' (Acts xvii. 23.)

URIM. Light.

The rabbins believed that the stones in the breastplate of the high-priest had supernatural illumination, but Christian Science reveals Spirit, not matter, as the illuminator of all. The illuminations of Science give us a sense of the nothingness of error, and they show the spiritual inspiration of Love and Truth to be the only fit preparation for admission to the presence and power of the Most High.

VALLEY. Depression; meekness; darkness.

'Though I walk through the valley of the shadow of death, I will fear no evil.'" (Psalm xxiii. 4.)

Though the way is dark in mortal sense, divine Life and Love illumine it, destroy the unrest of mortal thought, the fear of death, and the supposed reality of error. Christian Science, contradicting sense, maketh the valley to bud and blossom as the rose.

WILL. The motive-power of error; mortal belief; animal power. The might and wisdom of God.

'For this is the will of God.' (I Thessalonians iv. 3.)

Will, as a quality of so-called mortal mind, is a wrong-doer; hence it should not be confounded with the term as applied to Mind or to one of God's qualities.

WIND. That which indicates the might of omnipotence and the movements of God's spiritual government, encompassing all things. Destruction; anger; mortal passions.

The Greek word for 'wind' (*pneuma*) is used also for 'spirit', as in the passage in John's Gospel, the third chapter, where we read: 'The wind [*pneuma*] bloweth where it listeth. ... So is every one that is born of the Spirit [*pneuma*].' Here the original word is the same in both cases, yet it has received different translations, as in other passages in this same chapter and elsewhere in the New Testament. This shows how our Master had constantly to employ words of material significance in order to unfold spiritual thoughts. In the record of Jesus' supposed death, we read: 'He bowed his head, and gave up the ghost'; but this word 'ghost' is *pneuma*. It might be translated 'wind' or 'air', and the phrase is equivalent to our common statement, 'He breathed his last.' What Jesus gave up was indeed air, an etherealized form of matter, for never did he give up Spirit, or Soul.

WINE. Inspiration; understanding. Error; fornication; temptation; passion.

Index of Subjects

Academics 35, 59, 63, 86, 140, 160
accusation 13, 27, 78, 119, 137
alkaloid 34
American Transcendentalists 5, 6, 26, 41, 42, 58, 60
Ancient Greece 54
antipathy 19
antibacterials 51
A Philosophical Investigation of Christian Science 3, 36, 173
aprioristic, the 160
atheism 40, 137, 176
axioms 1, 65, 66, 71, 79, 81, 90, 91, 113, 118, 132, 144, 161, 162

Berkeley 16n5, 17, 22, 24-26, 57, 66, 67, 89
Bible 15, 32, 35, 38, 42, 69, 70, 89, 113, 117, 162, 165
biographer 50
biology 8, 47, 86, 152, 158
blasphemy 177
Boston 47, 49
Boston University 36
British Idealists 2, 12, 61, 94, 95, 125
Buddhism 6, 19

calculus, integral 121
cholera 153, 157
Christian Science church 2, 33, 34, 45, 46, 49, 68, 85, 147
Christian Science Journal 44, 155
Christian Science Practitioner 48, 91, 162
Christian Science Versus Pantheism 15, 27, 71, 77, 79, 82, 87, 137
Christian Science: Its Encounter with American Life 49, 50, 61
Christian Scientist Holocaust, The 144
churches 5, 23, 26, 27, 35, 137
combinations 111
combustion 76
Committee on Publication 49
contagion 156, 158
corporeality 84, 101, 178
COVID-19 56, 85, 147-151, 158, 159

death 17, 24, 31, 32, 34, 41, 51, 59, 65, 79, 82, 86, 88-90, 94, 95, 104-106, 113, 118, 122, 138, 149, 150, 153, 160, 162-164, 166, 175, 176, 178-184
devil 84, 163, 177, 178
Dial, The 42, 71
disease 17, 31, 138, 150-153, 157, 158, 166
Divine Truth 22, 52
domain 99, 100
drugs 137, 157, 164
duality 117, 118

Each Mind a Kingdom 37
Emergence of Christian Science in American Life, The 36
end times 116
esophagus 153
exegesis 25, 28
experiment 52, 66, 90-92, 113, 118, 151, 152, 156, 157, 160
everything 133

falsehoods 13, 69
Father-Mother 96
fideism 165
Fordham University 50

gender 102
gold 11, 62, 92
Gottschalk 2n1, 3, 4, 13n22, 19n18, 20n22&n28, 36, 43, 45n26, 56n14, 67, 70, 77
Green 61

Harvard University 49, 60
Herald of Christian Science, The 155
Hinduism 5, 19, 20, 27
Holy Ghost 27-29, 107, 179
Holy Spirit 27-29, 54, 89, 109, 144
Hypothesis 11, 23, 58, 66, 76, 90, 91, 113, 118, 137, 141

idealists 2, 7, 12, 13, 16, 18, 19, 59, 61, 63, 94, 95, 125
infinite 3, 25, 27, 30, 32, 38, 60, 66, 72, 73, 79, 87, 89, 95, 96, 98, 101, 102, 108, 114-116, 118, 120-124, 127, 130, 132-137, 141, 142, 161, 162, 166
infinity 27, 108, 115, 118, 121-123, 141, 144, 162
injustice 2, 9, 11, 21, 29, 149
institution 2, 21, 149, 177
intelligence 18, 66, 73, 76, 82, 145, 176-181

Jainism 20
Jesus 26-28, 33, 52, 77, 78, 84, 85, 96, 98, 101, 117, 176, 178, 180, 184
Journal of Christian Science 44
Journal of the American Medical Association 152
Justification 10, 18, 23, 46, 61

Katherine's Sheaves 46
Kingdom 33, 39, 116, 165, 166, 176, 180, 181
Knowledge 3, 19, 24, 27, 32, 38, 48, 58, 73, 89, 91, 95, 102, 103, 139, 142, 176, 180, 182

language 4, 7, 8, 11, 12, 61, 70, 75, 80, 165
least part 51, 53
Lord 48, 144, 175

Lynn, Mass., USA 2

magisteria 35, 56, 106, 110, 165
materia medica 147
materialism 6, 13, 36, 54-56, 87
Mary Baker Eddy: The Years of Authority 47, 49
Mary Baker Eddy: The Years of Discovery 47, 49, 50
Mary Baker Eddy: The Years of Trial 47, 49
Massachusetts Academy of Christian Science 43
millennialism 38, 39
miracles 42, 60, 181
Miscellaneous Writings, 1883-1896 4, 15, 71, 78, 79, 82, 84
mis-framing 1

Nature of Existence, The 12, 25, 61, 126-129, 161
New England 6, 26, 39, 52
New Testament 28, 45, 184
No and Yes 30, 78, 79, 82, 83
Nonexistence 9, 26, 30, 34, 40, 101, 102, 105, 113, 148, 151, 161

occasionalism 141, 142
omnipotence 86, 89, 90, 108, 118, 183
originality 10, 21, 36, 39, 41, 42, 63, 91, 146

pandemic 56, 85, 147, 148, 150, 154
paradox 9, 89, 113, 114, 120-122, 126, 162
paradigm 16, 99
Paradox of the Stone 85
People's Idea of God, The 15, 71, 78
perception 19, 25, 55, 61, 70, 75, 104, 114, 126, 127, 136, 139, 162, 163
PhD 3, 7, 12, 36, 38, 152, 173
phlogiston 76
placebo 92, 152
postmillennialism 39
Ptolemaic Model 76
prayer 16, 19, 34, 64, 66, 163, 165
premillennialism 39
preterism 39
problems 2, 8, 9, 23, 32, 47, 67, 69, 70, 88, 89, 92, 113-116, 120, 124, 132, 135, 139-142, 145, 153, 160, 162-164

Index of Subjects

publications 3, 12, 24, 30, 49, 63, 78, 94, 95, 117, 131, 152
Quality 6, 45, 46, 75, 83, 137, 183
radium 51
ratio 176
Reading Room 44
reinterpretation 21
religion 1, 2, 5, 9, 15, 19, 23, 29, 30, 42, 48, 106, 113, 137, 138
Religious Studies 29
Research 3, 9, 10, 35, 42, 49, 50, 63, 140, 165
Revelation 39
revelation 32, 33, 38, 95, 96, 101-103, 114, 116, 143, 144, 161, 181
Roman Catholic Church 26
romanticism 6
'r' 121, 122
Rudimental Divine Studies 15, 30, 71, 77, 79, 82
Russell's Paradox 114

SARS-CoV2 147-149
science of being 52, 65, 177
Science and Creation 93
selves 128
sensa 131
set theory 116
sickness 31, 66, 83, 84, 105, 117, 118, 122, 135, 164, 175, 178-182
Sikhism 20
Spanish Influenza 85, 147, 148, 150, 151, 154, 155, 158, 159
suffering 2, 5, 24, 26, 34, 40, 51, 153, 163
Swedenborgianism 19

taxonomy 21
textbook 4, 77
theodicy 23, 42
theology 4, 5, 10-13, 18, 23, 29, 35, 39, 41, 44, 45, 64, 65, 69, 72, 77, 81, 93, 104, 107, 115, 116, 137, 140, 146
'The Herald of Christian Science' 155
The Sophistries of Christian Science' 60
'Theology as an Empirical Science' 93
Tooth 85, 144, 145
toothache 85, 144

Unitarians 42, 60
United States of America *see USA*
'Unity of Good' 15, 30, 71, 77, 79, 82
USA 14, 15, 29, 45
'Upanishads' 5, 41

vacuum 100, 119
virus 148, 149, 153, 156, 158
vision 40, 140, 142, 179

Wissenschaftslehre' 58
woman 4, 32, 33, 35, 37, 44, 142, 180
'World Parliament of Religions' 29

X-rays 92, 93

zealousness 144
zeitgeist 18
zenith 128
Zeno's Paradox 120, 121
zero 115, 121, 122

Index of Names

Achilles 120-122
Alcott, B. 5, 6, 54, 55
Alcott, L.M. 5
Anaximander 119
Anaximenes 119
Aquinas 52
Aristotle 99, 100
Armstrong 24
Astor N. 34, 48

Barth, K. 45
Beauvoir, de S., 108
Bergmann, G. 144, 145
Bowen, F. 61
Braden, C.S. 50
Bradley, F.H. 20, 28, 61, 75, 128
Braude, A. 39
Burnet, J. 123
Butler, J. 108, 109

Cantor, G. 115
Carlyle, T. 59
Clemens, C. S. 5
Coleridge, T. 60
Cousin, V. 60
Cunningham, R.J. 50

Derrida, J. 108
Descartes, R. 140
Dickson, C. 50
Dyck, C. J. 50

Edwards, J. 18, 39
Einstein, A. 20, 44
Elwes, R. H. M. 133

Emerson, R. W. 5, 6, 26, 41, 55, 60
Euclid 134
Evans, W.F. 5-7, 18, 37, 38

Farnsworth, E. C. 60, 144
Fichte, J.G. 3, 12, 16, 18, 19
Findlay, J. 50
Foucault, M. 108
Fox, G. 136
Freud, S. 108

Gill, G. 6, 50, 51
Gorgias 40

Hanna, S.J. 33
Henry I, King 126
Henry, M. 28, 29, 36, 126
Hopkins, E.C. 44, 45, 164
Huttig, W. 156

Ingle, L.H. 136, 137, 158
Irigaray, L. 108

Jesus 26-28, 33, 52, 77, 78, 84, 85, 96-98, 101, 117
John (St.) 138, 161
Julian of Norwich 142, 143, 144

Kant, I. 17, 58
Kristeva, J. 108

Lacan, J. 108
Lipton, B. 152, 154
Londe, S. 154

MacIntosh, D.C. 72, 91, 93, 94
Malebranche, N. 140-142, 145
Marty, M. 50

Index of Names

McCracken, C. 140
McTaggart, J.M.E. 125-131, 134, 142, 144, 146
Meador, C. 153
Melissus 123-125
Meredith, G. 49
Mesmer, F. 181
Messenger, F. 39

Milmine, G. 43
Moore, G.G. 25

Nadler, S.M. 140
Newton, I. 121
Novalis 12, 23, 59

Parker, T. 42
Parmenides 107, 119, 120
Pasteur, L. 153
Peel, R. 8, 47-51, 53-56
Peppers-Bates, S. 140
Pickford, M. 34
Plato 117, 118
Pseudo-Dionysus 116

Queen Matilda 126
Queen Victoria 126

Quimby, P. 2, 5, 7, 17, 18, 37, 43

Rucker, R. 116

Satter, B. 37, 39
Schmaltz, T.M. 173
Sheldon, G. 46
Sheldrake, P. 173
Spinoza, B. 72, 84, 89, 131-136, 138, 139, 145
Steiger, H.W. 3, 12, 36, 51, 70, 74

Thales, 119
Thomas, H.D. 5
Thoreau, T.F. 5
Torrance, 72, 91, 93, 94
Twain, M. 4, 40, 42

Von Hardenberg 12, 23, 41, 59
Voorhees, A. 37-39

Walton, C. 140
Watson, J.B. 87
Wiggin, H.J. 63
Wittig, M. 108
Wolcott, P.C. 17
Woodbury, J. 43

Zeno 120 ff.

You may also be interested in:
Some Things Considered
A Selection of Essays of Biblical and Historical Significance
Bryan W. Ball

In *Some Things Considered*, Bryan Ball offers his readers a unique selection of distinctive essays on topics of theological and historical significance. Designed as stand-alone essays, across the volume Ball nevertheless explores the core beliefs fundamental to Christianity and key principles of biblical interpretation, allowing readers to come to his later chapters with a thorough grounding in biblical theology and interpretation.

Ball then explores a variety of topics, from the geological and geophysical evidence of the Genesis Flood to the seventeenth century controversy about the Sabbath day. Honing in on oft-misunderstood verses such as Daniel 8:14 and Genesis 1:16, he offers nuanced interpretations. He culminates the collection with a discussion of the biblical context surrounding the 'The Decline of the West'.

> *A very thoughtful read which has provoked me to be more careful in my interpretation of God's Word.*
> - **James Huzzey**, Retired pastor and Youth Minister

Bryan W. Ball is an Adventist, and retired academic and church administrator. He is the author of numerous books, including *The Seventh-Day Men* (2009), *The English Connection* (second edition, 2014), and *The Soul Sleepers* (2008). He holds a PhD from the University of London and has contributed to the *Oxford Dictionary of National Biography* and the *Encyclopaedia of World Faiths*.

Published 2024
Hardback ISBN: 978 0 227 18050 1
Paperback ISBN: 978 0 227 18043 3
PDF ISBN: 978 0 227 18049 5
ePub ISBN: 978 0 227 18048 8

You may also be interested in:
Blind Evolution

The Nature of Humanity and the Origin of Life
David Frost

In *Blind Evolution?: The Nature of Humanity and the Origin of Life*, Professor David Frost challenges the dominant worldview derived from Darwin's evolutionary theories and perpetuated in Richard Dawkins's atheistic propaganda for Neo-Darwinism: that our universe has 'at bottom, no design, no purpose, no evil and no good, nothing but blind, pitiless indifference'.

Frost deploys recent findings from a range of scientific studies that shake Neo-Darwinism to its foundation. Citing entertaining examples, from the inner workings of a single cell to the animal kingdom at large, from elephants and giraffes to the Japanese pufferfish, Frost maintains that Darwinian premises are wholly inadequate to engage with life or to provide a framework for our experiences of joy and sorrow, the problem of suffering, and the stark realities of good and evil.

Reflecting on the nature of existence, Frost points to a mode of human understanding parallel to scientific enquiry through the path of 'vision' accessed via the nous (or spiritual intellect). He argues that 'vision' is as much essential to our understanding of creation as is scientific enquiry – reality is best approached through a complementary partnership of both.

Professor David Frost has lectured and broadcast on literature and theology in two hemispheres and in seven countries. He was a lecturer at the University of Cambridge for ten years before taking up a Chair of English Literature in the University of Newcastle, NSW, where he remained for twenty-one years.

Published 2019
Hardback ISBN: 978 0 227 17696 2
Paperback ISBN: 978 0 227 17711 2
PDF ISBN: 978 0 227 906910
ePub ISBN: 978 0 227 90692 7